ERIC DUPRE'

THE LOST ART OF FAITH

ERIC DUPRE'

THE LOST ART OF FAITH

Copyright © 2018 by ERIC DUPRE.

All rights reserved. No part of this publication may be reproduced, distributed, or transmitted in any form or by any means, including photocopying, recording, or other electronic or mechanical methods, without the prior written permission of the author, except in the case of brief quotations embodied in critical reviews and certain other non-commercial uses permitted by copyright law.

Ordering Information: Quantity sales. Special discounts are available on quantity purchases by corporations, associations, and others. Orders by U.S. trade bookstores and wholesalers.

www.DreamStartersPublishing.com

ERIC DUPRE'

Table of Contents

The Lost Art of Faith 4
Preface 5
The "Game" of Life 11
The Power of Faith X=? Faith=Success 20
Designed Failures 24
The Two of You: The Inner You and the Outer You 29
How to Decode the Bible's True Power 33
Struggling Child 43
Inner-Child Development 47
Your Home 50
Know Thyself & Control Thyself 61
Needs Versus Wants 69
Struggling Through Any Process: "No Pain, No Gain" 75
Key Ingredients: Mind, Body, Spirit 90
Superhuman Behavior/Breaking Yourself 94
Spiritual Realm 3rd Dimension 101
My Inspiration 107
The Pyramid of Life Concept 110
Mental Preparedness for Life 113
Patterns 119
Bad Programming Equals Bad Output, Every Time 126
Selling Your Soul 131
Final Thoughts and Conclusion 136

The Lost Art of Faith

How to decode yourself & biblical scripture
To harness real lasting power
Know thyself & Control thyself

X

X=?

X=TRUTH

X=SUCCESS

FAITH=SUCCESS

How to transform your mind, body, and spirit using logical, faith-based doctrine
How to unlock and decode yourself using biblical, faith-based principles
How to hack into yourself, rewire yourself, and decode yourself

The key to a successful life starts here!

ERIC DUPRE'

Preface

This book is a ride-along journey of a series of collective thoughts, truths, concepts, opinions, and of inner and outer self-discovery as it pertains to solving the equation of a successful life by transforming your mind, body, and spirit, and opening up the doors you desire in life. Many people want success in different ways, but ultimately, we want a successful life with purpose and meaning. Fulfillment is the end game.

It's my hope that you learn, reinforce, and grow from what I'm about to share with the world for the first time in my life, about my own personal experiences and findings on this subject.

Life events and struggles don't come with a schedule or calendar, so with that said, this book's message is written the same way: in an un-sequenced order. Why? Because in the end, you have to do this yourself. I can only bring you to the door. The rest will be up to you, by your own choices, and the amount of effort you feel it's worth to you. The beauty of this book is that you can re-read any part or skip over other parts. If you've spent any time in biblical scripture, it's very similar to that. I like to pattern other successful things I find in life.

THE LOST ART OF FAITH

General Patton was quoted as saying: "If everyone is thinking alike, then somebody isn't thinking."

It's rare to see unique thinking in the world today because we are damn near like ants following patterns. Every now and then someone breaks out. For various reasons, some people see the world in the reverse order of how it should be, and their perception is not the same. Thus, they are forced to function and exist in a world that seems to contradict itself. I want you to keep this paragraph in mind from start to finish of this book. In the end, when you come back to this paragraph, you will understand this meaning in a new way.

A this moment in history, a paradigm shift in thinking and awakening is upon us as the explosion of information through open-source technology is flooding mankind, and it is, in my opinion, overwhelming our ability to keep up because the internet was that mega paradigm shift. We can get results or information without learning how to solve an actual problem. When power from knowledge is passed along without the experience of hard work or effort, the power will be abused, as it was not earned or fully understood.

This results in this performance rat race we try to live in is mentally unhealthy. To refocus, this book is part of the solution to counter this paradigm shift that will lead back to the fundamental core principles of life. When technology surpasses humanity, we will have a problem. We are already having problems, but that does not mean we can't solve problems. We can!

Systematic symptoms of a broken and failing society are no *one's* fault. They are our fault as a collective group of humans, as this is our society, and we need to own it. Good or bad, it's our world.

Taking a word problem and converting it to a solvable formula is what I'm aiming to do in this book. I took this approach from Sherlock Holmes who was great as solving complex problems by finding the true root cause and answer. If we don't get to the root, we spin our wheels.

In algebra, we are taught to solve for X when finding the absolute answer. To break down the most complex equation and solve for X, which, if correct, works every time you plug in the correct number. Everyone, or should I say most everyone, wants to be successful at something, and the reason for that is we need reason and purpose to find joy and fulfillment in life. If we can find that what we truly desire is to understand how to have a successful life that we can maintain for the entirety of our life. Ultimately, we just want to have a successful life, and we want to know how to achieve that.

From the dawn of man, this internal desire to find peace, love, joy, purpose, and meaning is man's ultimate quest in life. We individually struggle and chase this powerful three-letter word: "Why?" It's powerful, and it's what truly drives us as humans. Men have obtained almost everything a man could obtain and have not gotten any closer to the truth of the ultimate "Why?" Why are we here, and why am I here? What's my true purpose and meaning of why I was created? Some think about this; some don't care; some have given up trying to figure it out.

When you can solve this equation for yourself, you can start to live with fulfillment, purpose, peace, love, and joy, so you can enjoy the success in your life. The real beauty is that it is completely different for everyone, and each journey is unique, but at some point, we will all arrive at an absolute truth.

The purpose of the book is to share my personal experiences as a boy, son, grandson, student, father, husband, ex-husband, friend, co-worker, businessman, teacher, and at the core, just a man. After reading other books about success, they all centered on the success of a single topic or aspect of life. Here, through this short book, using biblical structure—aka, the living word of God—I'm attempting to help you transform yourself through decoding in a self-revealing process of your current state of mind, with the intention to bring you to a place where you have control over your life.

ERIC DUPRE'

The lost art of faith is not to be confused with lost religion, but the true connection between us and our creator is missing. When we drift farther from our creator, I assume that naturally, he also loses faith in us. That seems pretty logical. It's no different than when we drift away from someone we're in a relationship with. When they or we drift away from lack of effort, care, and love, people tend to leave others in search of someone who will give them attention, love, respect, and acknowledgement.

We place God on an unhuman level, but he's very much human when it comes to us caring and loving him—just how any real father would be. Just because you can't see him doesn't mean he doesn't exist. You can't see feelings of love in your heart, but your emotional heart hurts when someone doesn't love you. Keep this in mind as well as you read this book. It's key.

Personally, I'm a lazy man to your benefit, which means I want to get to the point and find what actually works in the fastest way possible. So, when we say lazy, others may say genius! I'll always take "genius" over "lazy" from someone else any day. Cajuns like to use the KISS method: Keep It Simple Stupid! With all that said, once you read this book, it will open your heart, spirit, and your mind, and you won't look at this world or your life the same ever again.

To what degree?

THE LOST ART OF FAITH

That will totally depend on your ability to identify with real truth, and how open your mind is to accepting something new or opposite of what you may currently believe. I'll say this: I respect everyone's thoughts and opinions, and many people's tiny influences have shaped and molded my beliefs. But ultimately, the experiences and the facts that I have gathered on Earth for thirty-nine years have formulated a life equation and message I want to share with you for your benefit . . . or entertainment. (Or both. Who knows?) I will and can only make one real promise to the reader: It will be interesting.

Enjoy the show!

Albert Einstein once said, "It's not that I'm so smart, it's just that I stay with problems longer." Think about his *time* and *effort* and how he earned his knowledge. The result of his dedication to such complex problems he solved shifted the entire world.

Thirty-nine years, folks. That's 14,235 days. One might say this is my life's work, and it truly is. If I were obtaining my master's degree, this would be my thesis paper. I hope you find it to be well worth reading, and I hope it's published before I'm forty and am considered "old."

Chapter 1

The "Game" of Life

I was told by a publisher that for any book, story, or movie to be believable, meaningful, and successful, you need a main character and to help the reader solve a problem. You to know this character's background, who he is, where he comes from, *who* he comes from, and why the hell he even matters. So here we go. . . .

My name is Eric Dupre'. I was born an hour south of Dallas in Kaufman, Texas, to Jackie, a seventeen-year-old girl from South Louisiana who lived with her mother and father, EJ and Geneva. EJ was an oilman by trade and worked on rigs and in construction. He was a father of five kids: two boys and three girls. A hard worker, he fought in WWII as a navy man and was respected and highly regarded for his loving, caring, and honorable ways.

My grandmother was in charge of raising the kids and taking care of the household. She was barely five feet but tough like Granny from *The Beverly Hillbillies*. Grandpa made enough money to provide what was needed and then some; they were middle class, you could say. Family was everything to them. My mother was a young, beautiful teenager full of glowing life, the youngest of five and the apple of my grandpa's eye.

When he found out his youngest innocent daughter was pregnant in high school, I'm sure it destroyed his heart knowing what struggles lay ahead of her and having her youth taken away. My father was not ready to be a father, so my grandparents moved my mother from South Louisiana to Texas to get away from him. They didn't want my mother and father to marry and ruin everyone's lives because a mistake had been made. I don't want to sound harsh, but it was a mistake. I was a mistake, and I was brought into this world in the summer of 1979.

Prior to my birth, my grandparents went to my sixteen-year-old mother and placed my life in her young hands. "You can have him adopted, you can keep him, or we'll help you raise him."

Had she chosen one of those, we wouldn't be talking about failure because I wouldn't even be here. How's that for some purpose? She chose the hardest journey of all the routes—to give birth and raise a child as a child—a sacrifice for me to have a chance at being something in this world.

ERIC DUPRE'

Right out the gate, my life was complicated. Within a few months of my birth, we all moved back to Lafayette, Louisiana. My grandfather became my father, grandfather, and best friend. I don't know any child who had that much love poured into him by another human being. At the age of four, my world and my best friend came to an end at the hands of a massive heart attack. I sat front row at the funeral and walked up to him. I looked at my mother and told her to wake him up. "Why doesn't he just wake up?" You can't explain to a four-year-old that he ain't gonna wake up, as death isn't a reality yet—until it is.

For the first time in my life, I felt the emotions of great loss and pain, and I was confused about why I was crying. I cried, and that was it. I'd just lost what I loved the most in the entire world.

Emotional damage occurs when we are attacked and crushed by life's lessons. Life can come at us hard and fast. As I write this, knowing my four-year-old self had to start battling life at such a young age makes me tear up.

These kinds of experiences start to shape and mold us during the course of our entire lives. My grandmother couldn't raise me on her own, so my mother got me and started raising me. At the age of four, the concept of money, wealth, survival, mental health, eating right, religion, and God mean absolutely nothing. What *does* mean something to you at this age? Personal comfort, happiness, feeling safe, love, and joy—just to name a few. The basic things that will also become mega important to you once you get past all the BS distractions in life are human touch, affection, love, and being you without judgment or punishment.

A verse in the Bible states that we should be "in the world, but not of it." Humans start to conform to a world based on what society has a habit of doing, by copying behaviors we often see and learning by sight because at early stages we can't communicate verbally. Some things aren't learned; they are part of our DNA. You don't teach a baby to eat, sleep, breathe, and so forth. This DNA code is part of the subconscious brain, which is hardwired into us.

During the early stages of life, we have to be careful because some programming gets wired into our subconscious and later arises in our youth or adult stages. At this point, tapping into that subconscious can be extremely hard to change. This just goes to show you how life molds us but does not define us.

Change is the one constant in life, but at some stage for humans, it can be the most difficult thing to do or accept. If you haven't noticed by now, this book is not your standard format, so it will jump around from personal stories to diving into some deep thinking and observations of my own knowledge and firsthand experiences. I'm not programmed to conform to a structured thinking process. To be honest, the world around us is so structured, so to follow patterns and conform to it stands to reason that it was designed this way. It's a form of control to keep things in "order." Order is what makes people feel consistent, structured, and safe. As adults and folks who have experienced enough in life, we know that's an illusion. As much as a we accept life on a daily basis, we often don't think or spend much time on death. There is a beginning and ending, just like this book, and so will our journey be in life.

The patterns of life are mirrored all around us. Fear is tied to death because of the unknown—not really death itself. Anything that once lived will also surely end. When something ends, does it truly end, or does it just become something else or go somewhere else? The *when* and the *how* are what keep us thinking about it. I personally feel that there is an afterlife, so death does not scare me as much as most. To be honest, I feel that something far better exists beyond life on Earth.

With all that said, what does any of this have to do with being a failure? Failure isn't the bad part; it's the fear of failure and then the fear of you *being* a failure in your life's purpose. A little deeper . . . How do you truly know you're fulfilling your purpose? Do we get a letter in the mail or any real confirmation?

Expectations from outside forces can kill a person's self-esteem based on a comparison of measurable performances. Who in the hell has the authority or right to dictate these things upon other humans? If you're over the age of twenty-one, the words *fair* and *equal* are just words. Who you are born to, how much money you have, and what position of authority you have, can and will, without a doubt, dictate your level of measurable success. Your ability to work within the confines of the rules and laws of our society, aka "the game," will also determine your levels of success in a controlled society. We are not created equal, nor are we born in an equal starting position in the game. So, "failure" within this dynamic is a subjective term. Some have to start twenty miles from the starting line and others one mile.

What I want you to know is that the comparison will not often be a fair measurement of success and failure. Life is not designed to be fair. It's a random game of chance in which all the players (humans), at some point, must define their own rules or be subjected to a very cruel, unfair game. We are told things are fair, but clearly they are not. This is where perspective will once again come into play. The more perspective from experiences you have, the better you will tilt your odds of playing or outplaying the field.

"Break the rules, not the law, but break the rules." —Arnold Schwarzenegger

If you play by the house rules of life, you'll often lose. The house rules are designed for the house to win, not you. Trying to outsmart, outthink, or outhustle is possible, but you can and will burn out quickly. Faith or God's plan now enters the conservation. God, aka the Creator, must have created you for a purpose. Your free will allows you to choose infinite choices, and you must find the one that is right for you so you can gain your personal fulfillment, enlightenment, and purpose. This may be the million-dollar question, or nowadays, the billion-dollar question: Shall one seek the glory of himself among men, or seek that which glorifies God our creator in front of men? How do we know what that even is? This makes failure even more extreme because it's one thing to be a failure to yourself, society, or others . . . but to fail God?

I honestly think God built all this stuff for everyone to enjoy and share collectively. We aren't all equal, and this forces us into action. When one man is poor, it paves the way for another man to be charitable. It's a balance of yin and yang or day and night. One can't exist without the other. Historically, all nations rise and fall because none has yet to achieve this concept of "one." It's an all-or-nothing buy-in from society; a society which bounds its principles to the biblical doctrine of a righteous way of living. Scripture states that we are all like various parts of the body, that no one part is any more or any less important to function as a complete body. The hand does not work without the arm, the arm without a shoulder, and so forth.

Knowing we are all somehow interconnected by something we can't see or explain doesn't mean we aren't connected. Proof that humans are connected is that on billions and billions of planets, we currently have only found humans on one. Now, science's law of averages tells us that there should be other planets with humans, but there aren't. This yields a conclusion that we are meant to be on the planet together for a purpose and reason, in relationship with one another. I feel this creates more combinations of new events and new discoveries. If we can accept that we are as one, and we rise and fall together, we must also accept we can succeed and fail together.

Why do we place so much power on individual success? When one rises, someone falls. When someone profits a monetary gain, he finds a way to sell at a higher value. I assume that is why "In God We Trust" is printed on our U.S. currency. Why am I spilling out these various dynamics that appear to be all over the place? Because feeling like a failure doesn't come from one source; by design, it is all over the place. Failure creates lots of negative human emotions—shame, guilt, feeling like a lesser being. We are in Satan's paradise at this moment, which means we're overloaded with more selfish options that distract us from the true focus of love, passion, family, purpose, meaning, and being.

I think people feel more like a failure now than in any time in history. Why? Simply, we have more people on this planet, and people are power. The distance between the haves and have-nots is gaping, and with the ability to speed things up with technology, we've become a society that is no longer at peace. We aren't easily satisfied anymore. We need more and more, and we need it faster and faster.

Social media and retail have joined forces to penetrate our personal lives and keep us from reaching levels of satisfaction because it's good for bottom line quarterly profits. Damn near everything is monetized. We are living in a virtual reality, and it keeps us in a suspended, unsatisfied place that makes us feel like we need to buy more stuff to feel successful or adequate. We need the opposite emotion of what failure creates. We need success, hope, love, passion, accomplishment, and to feel valued. These tangible feelings are some of the most powerful forces. They are the real horsepower of the human engine that feeds your spirit and enhances performance.

Chapter 2

The Power of Faith X=? Faith=Success

Faith equals success might sound stupid, but once you've read this book, come back to this chapter and see if you look at your faith and the power of faith in the same way. When most people hear about faith, they don't automatically associate it with success or think in terms of how it equates to good business practices.

Let's define the word *faith* and how it's used in this book. Faith is a set of your beliefs, your own grounding values and principles through your actions in life. When you break down the heart of life, it boils down to your ability to have solid and healthy relationships with others. In order for you to have this great, healthy relationship, you need to have a foundational framework that keeps your overall well-being in harmony.

Having this great aura surrounding you is a vibrant feeling of positive, reflected energy. This type of presence from a person is very attractive and allows others to feel at peace. Obtaining this aura through faith is the cornerstone in building a great person who builds many great relationships throughout life. This leads to a successful life at every level. In my opinion, this is becoming a lost art in Western culture due to many breakdowns in our current society.

Maintaining a well-balanced, harmonized mind, body, and spirit is the pathway for personal success, and it only happens when interlinked with others who share this partnership as part of a universal connection. It creates a strong bond. The gravitational field of attraction for folks who emit this aura deeply connects them. You'll often hear the term *like-minded people*. When you're on the same wavelength, it's a good sign that you have a high level of peace about the connection and relationship with another.

The physical world is the one we can see, and the metaphysical is the unseen world that surrounds us. We can feel its presence and power. The more tuned in you are with a healthy mental state of mind, the more you'll feel this force. Faith-based principles from Judeo-Christian texts can unlock many of man's untapped powers. I will share my own personal thoughts, opinions, experiences, and research to shed some light on this subject. This is intended help you achieve a lifetime of success at all levels. In today's world, we have allowed many things to take the place of our faith and founding principles of life, which is causing a decline in overall happiness and health.

THE LOST ART OF FAITH

Come and take this journey with me of inner discovery and breakdown of my own story and accounts that have forever changed my mind and life on what a real successful life means in faith.

I wasn't always a person of faith. I was aware of it being raised as a Catholic, but the true power of faith was not revealed until I basically lost everything I loved in this world at the pinnacle of the highest level of success a man could have. I obtained a thriving business, marriage, kids, house, cars, and financial success. It was Heaven on Earth until I lost it all, and almost lost my life, within twenty-four months. I was forced to crack the code, so to speak, or terminate my life due to the pain of losing so much in life without understanding why. Living a hollow, empty life without true fulfillment is not a life, and that's what I was living. I tried amassing all those things because I thought it was the key to happiness.

The key relationship and the missing link were a relationship with my creator, established through faith, my true beliefs in action, by way of my own personal conduct of living. Faith has to become an action word—an active process. If faith just remains a belief with no actions, we will never access its real power for our lives. I will help direct you through this maze to show how I arrived at my understanding and assist you in achieving this great life-altering process. I'd been so systematically quantitative about obtaining results in life, it was hard to force my mind to open up to philosophical teachings that actually ended up being logically scientific. The principles of building good things that last end up following some of these universal principles: time, effort, and process.

Human beings are so complex, you have to merge multiple things as a package deal or there will be a huge disconnect on how all things work collectively in a harmonized life balance. If we obtain success but can't maintain or sustain it, what's the point? Don't we want a sustainable lifetime of success, not just a short burst of temporary success?

Chapter 3

Designed Failures

I am a Christian man and a man of faith with an independent, unique style, just like the other six or seven billion people on this planet. As a Christian man, I would then have to agree to be a judgmental man, a sinner, and a hypocrite as well. I'm not perfect, not even close, but the fact that I can be transparent and honest should tell you a lot about what me. This story is about my personal journey with failing at damn near everything I've ever done in life. I'm okay with it because I found out who the hell I am in all of this. It took me thirty-nine years, but as they say, better late than never.

I failed at jobs, relationships, marriage, business, school, religion, and most everything else you can think of. You could say I've mastered the art of failing. Worst of all, I failed at being me—yeah, the perfect imperfect screwed-up me, and I had to be happy with that dude. I had to burn the house to the ground and start over from scratch, ground zero, back to the drawing board. I had to undo and redo thirty-nine years of bad programming to reveal, heal, and rebuild me. I hated my life and who I had allowed myself to become. You can't escape "you" no matter how hard you try. A person might as well get real comfortable with themselves, as this world will not help with that one bit. A famous guy once said, "Know thyself." A not-so-famous guy (me) said, "Control thyself, because if you don't, no one else can do it for you, my friend."

This book is going to be very different from probably anything you've ever read. It's going to be raw, not very formatted, with random shorts stories, outside the box thoughts, and deep-thinking side notes. Can you imagine a bunch of yourselves from different times of your life all talking to you? The seven-, eighteen-, twenty-one, twenty-six, and thirty-nine-year-old you? Yeah, welcome to my world. Buckle up, because it's going to get interesting.

No one thinks all those "you's" are inside one person. Even the older you, along with your memories, thoughts, emotions, and experiences are inside of you all the time. What I've come to learn is what I thought was normal to me is not normal to others. I do not see the world like everyone else, so life has been extremely complex and difficult.

Dr. John Forbes Nash, a genius mathematician who suffered from mental illnesses, forced his mind to find solutions to complex math problems using a much different approach than his colleagues. This set him apart because his approach was from a nonlinear way of thinking. His weakness or illness ended up being his greatest strength and value. This book is a brand-new journey in which the reader will also be taking a new journey and exploring this information with me as I write this down for the very first time.

I don't fear things in the world because I control very little of it. I fear things inside myself. I have the ability to control many things within my mind, but within each mind are unlimited possibilities when fully unlocked. What's sad is, as kids you're taught that anything is possible and to dream big. As an adult, trying to break through, be something extraordinary, and make those big dreams come true, can get you ridiculed. We all know that the few people who make it big at some point are labeled crazy until they finally make it to where they are going. Some can see the beauty in your passion for seeking the success you want to obtain.

A. If I am all those things, then what shall I do? Just give up?
B. Or take all that stuff and become the best screwed-up, perfect version of me and press forward?

After thirty-nine years of fighting, wondering, being, failing, I rolled with B. If I had chosen A, I would have given up on the life that I truly wanted to live, and you'd never be reading any of this cool stuff. In my opinion, that would be a crying shame.

ERIC DUPRE'

In your life there are two of you: the internal you and the external you. Because of vulnerability, it takes a lot of courage to share the internal self with the rest of the world. I'm also one the most transparent humans on planet Earth. Hiding and lying have only hurt me, and I no longer wish to be hurt. I also seek the truth in all things. The truth shall always set you free. Yes, the truth hurts, but in the end, you either accept it or deny it. Either way it's still the truth. Your reality or perspective may not be the same as mine, yet we are looking at the same thing. During the course of this book, I'd like you to keep this perspective locked into your mind.

I'm writing this book because I know it will help people. At the same time, I don't care what anyone thinks about this book or of me. Honestly, those two things aren't what's most important. I love and respect people for different thoughts, opinions, ideas, colors, creeds, and tribes, and I respect and love myself as well. At the end of the day, we all have to live with ourselves and what we do here in this place in time. I'm a spiritual man of great biblical faith, but I don't brand my faith as a religion. It's 100% unique and authentic to me and my creator. Having faith is believing in something greater than yourself. This book is going to cover many things that just about every single human has struggled or thought about deeply at some point in life:

- Why am I here, what's my purpose?

- Who am I, and why am I important in all this?
- Faith, beliefs, religion, no religion
- Good, bad, evil, lucky, unlucky, fair, unfair
- The human mind and reality
- Science meets faith
- Me, the world or universe, and God

I am making this book personal so you know it's authentic and from a real dude who's not afraid to share his internal voice with others.

Chapter 4

The Two of You: The Inner You and the Outer You

When you have the courage to allow the authentic inner you to be revealed to the world, in all aspects of life, you will start to find your way and purpose. Let me add a key piece to that: it's when you allow the mature, experienced, wiser, authentic inner you to be revealed.

    We seem to keep the inner self locked up from the world. If we allowed our true thoughts and feelings to be expressed openly, would it not fit the mold of who we think we need to be? It's a mega fear for us to openly say and express how we truly think and feel on the inside. Society has its norms, and if you don't fit into those norms, you're weird, out of control, or bad. When we watch movies, the stars of those movies often don't hold back and express what they really think. It seems to make them funny, real, tough, or something other than weird. If I'm being honest, I have racing thoughts due to my dyslexia, and I have to control the hell out of my overthinking, what I say, and what I do twenty-four hours a day.

    Our minds have been filled with so much junk. We need to find a way to purge all that crap out and detox our brains. It took years of forcing myself to control this, but I hurt a lot of folks by my words. I sold it off to myself as "that's what I was honestly thinking." Bottom line, when it comes to success in life, we all have a ton of mental and physical challenges combined with moral codes, character, and social norms, balanced within whose expectations you want or need to please in order to get ahead. This is a lot to think about and control. If you have a good existing habit for all this, then great. You'll do great. If not, you will struggle your ass off when you're just being you.

    We all want to believe we can just be ourselves around others. We can be real, but that comfort zone and relationship just takes time to build. Being the authentic you around everyone isn't a novel idea until you've established a solid relationship. Some people flat out say what's on their mind: "Well, that's just me." If what you say is rude and crude, you're going have some issues, period. If you can start to articulate the same things with better word choices, you will do better. Ultimately, you need to create the habit of self-control.

Biblically, some of the worst things we do aren't even *what* we do, it's what we say to others. There are tons of scriptures about the tongue and how bad it can damage and/or kill relationships. When you speak without considering others, it can damage you. People cannot un-hear something. If what you said was harsh, you leave a sword in their hearts.

Back to the two "you's." The inner you might say I can do or be X, but the outer you doesn't match. This is a habit-forming part of the process of conquering fears and exhibiting courage. Take it one step at a time. Practice the inner you, in baby steps, until you feel more comfortable. Like anything else, the more you practice, the more comfortable you become, and your progression becomes exponential. Once you start to see and feel your transformation, you will enjoy the results and want to do it more. When you take the first initial leap of faith in life, you might just take off like a rocket. Your first step is huge; without it, nothing ever gets started. The sooner you move forward, the sooner you will be closer to becoming the inner you that you always wanted to be.

If the folks around you do not support you, then it's time to really evaluate those people. Tell them what it is that you want to do and become. No matter how crazy it is, they need to know what you really desire. You want what you want.

THE LOST ART OF FAITH

Don't ever let this world try to trick you out of that, because it will, and you'll believe it. Believe in yourself and start using your faith to help transform yourself and your life.

Once you realize you're a great person with a gift to share, you will have your confidence, aka swagger. This is your unique swagger, which doesn't have to look like Joe Cool Alpha Male's. You know what you know, and you're good at that. Have faith so you can handle what you need to handle. If you can show and communicate this to folks, you can establish a good relationship as well as create a level of trust. Then you'll be on the right path.

Build off of that and grow as little or as much as you can handle. Do everything in moderation, and in time, you will go a long way. Don't burn out and get overly excited. Remain calm and collected. Life is not a sprint, it's a marathon, so take your time and have patience. Control your race at your pace to stay within your current ability. If you get outside of that, you will have issues.

Chapter 5

How to Decode the Bible's True Power

The Bible is an amazing and powerful tool full of allegory, which means that some scripture has dual meaning or a deeper meaning than it first appears to have. Reading scripture as a child yields a basic simple story. As you get older and mature in life, that same story has a much deeper concept. This is why good pastors are very wise at pulling out the deeper story line. This just goes to show you how incredibly masterfully written the Bible is, especially in the time it was created, projecting into the future and seeing how these teachings are just as relevant today as they were two thousand years ago. Without question, we can understand that this is a special document written specifically for mankind.

THE LOST ART OF FAITH

No mortal human could have created such knowledge and understanding of mankind's need for faith as a necessary component to bringing forth purpose and meaning. It's a written guide and the ultimate how-to book. No other self-help book even comes close to the power of the holy Bible, which is why it has withstood the test of time. Truth and facts always withstand the test of time. A basic example would be:

Luke 6:31
"Do to others as you would have them do to you."

The Bible is full of thousands of one-liner clichés. Sayings that are rooted in as much solid fact and truth as a man could ever get. The lessons are simple, yet billions of people fall short of this simplicity every day. The lessons contain so much power if you can harness, believe, and live by this code as part of your core foundational principles.

Here's another breakdown of something simple, deeper, and important: *"Honor your father and your mother." (Exodus 20:12)* They didn't choose to say "become them" or "submit to them," but to "honor" them. This is a very clever word choice. Why? Because you might have had horrible parents who you don't love or like, but if you honor them by being a great human, you bring honor. It takes a bigger person to be better and honorable than their mother or father. It shows that you can still show respect even if you don't agree with or like them. You don't have to live their life; you get to choose to live a better one. God knew that in some cases we would not respect our parents for their own actions toward their children. Thus, we must learn to forgive past transgressions in order to grow in our faith.

Even the worst parents have created some of the very best humans on Earth, and they rose above their situation to become special individuals. Submitting to a higher authority is often part of life. If you can't accept that with your own parents, you will struggle with this later in life, work, school, society, and so forth. It's not because these people are always the best or have good intentions; it's because we have to learn to submit to many situations during the course of life. At some point you'll even have to submit to God, the highest authority. Knowing that as much as your pride and ego make you feel like you're in full control of everything, he has a way of bringing you to your knees in the blink of an eye.

No man can withstand the weight of the world, let alone the weight of his own world. We need other people from time to time, so learning how be obedient when you need help is a major sign of leadership. Getting the job done is more important than your pride. Just about every major culture on Earth would fully back this statement in reinforcing these ancient biblical teachings. I'm telling you, as you start to see how powerful this information is in unlocking your potential, you'll become amazed. Then you'll think, "Wow, this has been in front of my face the entire time, and I had no idea."

I'm going to clue you into something very important: Some of the greatest, most powerful things on planet Earth are right in front of your face—like the good book. When you are armed with this knowledge, you can do and overcome more than you could have ever imagined.

Look at the Bible in two ways: metaphorically and literally. Most people want to argue its stories and historical value. The reason it was written was for inspiration, very much like a modern-day movie that was written to speak to our core. At the time it was created, books were super rare and sacred, only for elite, highly-educated people. Once printing became available, more people read books like a modern-day laptop of information.

Bottom line: If you stop arguing the facts of the Bible and read the intent of the content, you'll obtain inspiration that will help guide you to a happy and successful life experience. The entertaining stories are not boring, so the reader stays engaged and learns the material. This is an impressive writing technique that everyone, two thousand years later, still replicates in books and movies. The important thing is what the book represents and what it teaches. Fact: None of us were around when any of these events took place. So, to argue about who, what, when, and where is unimportant versus understanding the point of *why* the book was written.

ERIC DUPRE'

The actual focus on the intent and its teachings are written for humanity. Why would someone compose such a book for us and ensure that through its writings and teachings, it would reach out to the entire world two thousand years later? Just by chance? Come on! It's because whatever created us knew we needed direction and instruction. When we have infinite choices in life, mankind requires structure and guidance.

We need something to point us in the right direction with challenges—or boundaries—for our own good. In exploring all major religious texts and core principles on how to live a good, successful life, it's my belief we share common ground. I personally choose Christianity even though groups have abused it historically, and all its followers are, at times, sinners and hypocrites. Most folks would say, "How dare you say such bad things about the Christian faith?" Well, it's true. A mature Christian would agree, as well. They'd also say: "That's the point. We are all imperfect, broken beings, which is why we need faith to help guide us for correction and reproof of living a successful life."

The biggest reason I'm 100% all in is because I have two children who I love more than anything in this universe. I would do anything for them—even give my own life. Christianity is the only religion in which a child (Jesus) was sacrificed for all of mankind to be saved by grace, not by our work here on Earth or because we are good to others. This is the greatest sacrifice that could have ever been willingly made by anyone on Earth.

    To become a true Christian, I had to ask myself if I could make such a sacrifice. That was the hardest realization I had to contemplate in my faith. Could I give up what I loved the most in this world to be allowed to live an eternal life in Heaven? This is the biggest and hardest test of faith. Within twenty-four months of asking that question, my wife divorced me and took my kids from me. Instead of becoming angry at God, I turned to him for answers, and the more I did, the more and more peace and understanding I gained. You see, everything, at some point here on Earth, will be taken from you, willingly or unwillingly. It's not because you're bad; it's because this is part of life. In an instant, one can lose everything in a fire, car wreck, and so forth. Our generation won't be the first or the last to forgo trials and tribulations. If you lose hope, faith—and possibly your soul—out of anger and rage, you will live a tormented life here on Earth. Readers, please let this sink into you: It's not *if*, it's *when*. If you don't mentally prepare and armor yourself with the words of God to keep you well grounded, you can and will be destroyed.

    Yeah sure, you get up every day and go to work and do a few things here and there, but you are hollow on the inside. You're just going through the motions. You truly aren't living, you're just surviving, and just surviving sucks! I learned the hard way and lost my family. I can never return home to them for the rest of my life. Without faith, there is no way a true loving father could survive that kind of hopeless despair.

I was in some of the darkest places after my loss. However, I always saw my children's faces in my mind, and they were my light. I army-crawled for months, going through depression, while begging my ex-wife to spare our family. As I grew weaker, she forced me to my knees to accept divorce. Being a man who could do nothing to save his kids from that kind of pain was one of the worst feelings a parent could endure. I tried lifting my entire world onto my back until I was crushed and forced to give up. I had to give it all to God. Only God has that kind of strength, and I experienced this the hard way. This is the moment I had to entrust him with my new life and start diving into my personal faith to understand why this had to happen to me.

This is why I am writing this book and you are reading it. This is my "Why?", and I finally got an answer to the reason this happened. It was to come out and share all this raw, personal, traumatic stuff. This is what I was forced to learn, and it's what I need to share with the world. I will not be the first man to go through traumatic life events, and I won't be the last, but for every man, woman, and child I can help with this book, I will. I want you to be as prepared on as many levels of mind, body, and spirit as possible so you can live with peace, love, and joy while you deal with life's roller coasters. **Remember: if it's good, it's a blessing, and if it's bad, it's just a lesson.**

All of this will take you far in life. Your positive outlook and attitude are what will make you stand out from the crowd and get you through a hard day. As others complain and moan when it's hard, you will keep your spirits up. Folks would rather be near a positive person than a negative individual who's lost and hurting.

"See, to survive is to suffer, but to live, well that's to find meaning in the suffering." DMX

Let's discuss where the authority of the good book's scriptures and lessons come from. Does the authority come from a king, a president, the Pope, a government official, the highest-ranking military official, your dad, your boss? No, it comes from none of these people. It comes from our creator. The Bible is completely free; it costs nothing. Yes, I get that people have profited from the good book for various reasons, but almost anywhere on Earth, this book and its teachings are 100% free or just the cost of the publishing.

The only time anyone can profit from you is when you choose to pay someone for something. When we find value in possessions, we don't mind paying for it. I personally have never attended a church that I had to pay at the door before I was allowed in. With the internet today, you have access to millions of resources to assist you. When you place the authority of teaching powers into someone else's hands, you have moved the control away from yourself to someone else. At some point, you have to learn how to teach yourself through reading material and understanding it, so you can apply it. The moment you depend on someone else is when you've created value to their ability to impart knowledge, thoughts, and/or beliefs to assist you. This is fine, but they will not be able to choose your life's path for you.

 The test of faith by your actions as a believer is one test in life you can't cheat or get assistance with. It's all you and your own will. Principles and faith are historically passed down from parent to child, but more so by example. As families are diluted or absent of parents, the principles and faith decline, year after year, until we live in a misguided society. It is and always will be our individual responsibility as adults to teach ourselves and our families scripture on a daily basis.

 You are your household's authority of the teachings in which you should teach and live by. Anything additional is an elective tool to assist you, but the obligation and duty is your own. Taking on this responsibility denotes a level of maturity in character and virtues.

 Again, faith will always lead you to a higher level of success once you start to see tangible results. Faith-based dynamics serve both Heaven and Earth dually, so it's a win-win once you believe.

Chapter 6

Struggling Child

In the United States, when we are young, we are told and taught we can be and do anything we want, at home and at school. Our minds run wild, we are creative, we ask why about everything, we see new things, and we learn new things. Our youth gets in to a structured educational system around the age of six. They stay in this system, by law, until about the age of seventeen. We are pretty much all taught the same exact things because of state and federal standards and basic formatted teaching. It's pretty simple and is designed with the needed structure to sustain and maintain the economic platform needed for this country. It's taught for the masses.

    The only reason I bring this up is because this format is in place by decision makers to maintain this society's business model that was here long before any of us arrived.

THE LOST ART OF FAITH

The sad thing is to have a competitive edge and ranking system. Kids and parents are only focused on the performance result—not on that lesson learned for a lifetime of support for basic fundamentals. Information is committed to short-term memory long enough to get the high test score, but then discarded to make room for the next test. If students were asked to recall this information for use later in life, they couldn't recall most of what was taught. Passing a test temporarily versus learning information that can help us down the road is vital to real education and development of any person.

    Both retaining foundational education and developing a strong mind are important. These are the building blocks of things to come in life, but as education gets advanced, it often gets harder. The struggle is the most important lesson, as this is what builds up true inner strength and character.

    Now I didn't have two full-time, supportive parents growing up. I had a struggling single mother working her tail off trying to figure out life on the fly. I went to the first open-concept elementary school in Texas, which basically meant no walls. I assume it's cheaper to build schools that way. There was a lot of student and teacher cross noise. My mind was always struggling to focus on my teacher or lesson while hearing three other classes at the same time. I excelled at math, science, and social studies, but I couldn't read for squat.

ERIC DUPRE'

In the mid-80s, doctors didn't really test kids for special needs like dyslexia because it really wasn't a thing. You were basically tossed into special needs classes. When we had to go to auditorium with my ESL class and the other classes saw me in that class, I felt ashamed. When I went on to regular level classes, I felt normal.

My mom worked so much, doing what she could to take care of our needs, but she didn't understand the depth of my struggle. But what could she do? They didn't understand or even identify my actual issue.

Dyslexia makes it super hard for children to learn phonics and to know that a shape has an assigned sound, and when combined with other shapes (letters), it forms a word. I looked at the entire word as a complete shape that made a sound. I basically memorized the entire word shape to know the sound it made. Out of shame and pain, I forced myself to get out of that ESL class and into regular-level classes where I made C's.

I didn't truly learn how to read until I got to junior high. This was the first time in my young life I had to fight like hell for something. At this point, you may be wondering if this book is about what you thought it was about: faith and success. If you know anything about great faith and success, then you know it normally starts with many massive failures. I'm going to share personal stories of my own life trials and tribulations and conclusions. These are life-building blocks, chapter by chapter, tying together thirty-nine years of life's research and development, all poured into one book that you can read in less than a week.

Chapter 7

Inner-Child Development

As the body grows from youth to adulthood, your outward appearance and size may change, but often the inner child hasn't matured at the same rate. Usually, this is from the lack of learning, experiences, and/or coaching. By the time you have aged to adulthood, you may or may not have had to truly struggle through life events, and the experience of that can be traumatic; you react like a child in an adult's body. I'm sure you see this all the time and wonder why they don't just grow up. Some people just don't know how to make that transition, so all their behavior seems childish. If someone had a bad childhood and didn't like the experience, their newfound control over this new adult life is the outlet for the inner child to experience the childhood they never had.

THE LOST ART OF FAITH

It is a huge thing for men to understand what it means to "man up"—especially when they just don't know how. Like getting coaching lessons, a new student wants to get better; it's the same thing for some men to "man up." If they didn't have a good consistent father or father figure in life, they more than likely won't have this skill. I was one of those men, and I had to act the part, which occasionally worked, until I truly needed to be a real man. In hard times, I just froze up and didn't know what the heck to do. I felt helpless and weak, especially when it came to my wife and kids.

"Brothers, do not be children in your thinking. Be infants in evil, but in your thinking be mature." (1 Corinthians 14:20)

When you control selfish childish desires and focus on greater priorities in life and placing them in the right order, that is the day you've crossed over from youth to adulthood. Makes sure the needs of your family and your faith, not self-glory, remain your focal point and come first over your own desires. If you screw up anything, don't screw up this priority; otherwise, you'll get sideways really quickly.

"But seek first the kingdom of God and his righteousness, and all these things will be added to you." —Jesus (Matthew 6:33)

This scripture is talking about seeking what is right first before considering only yourself and how something will profit your situation. If you choose to only consider yourself, relationships will terminate sooner than later, and you'll have a pattern of failed relationships in all aspects of life. The men who learn this seem to get everything because they know how to balance out, give and take, in personal and business relations. "He's not perfect, he just knows how to maintain stability in his relationships so both parties feel comfortable." There are those who know how to manipulate situations to get what they want. Then, there are those who are genuine and honest and know that the relationship means more than anything tangible they could gain for themselves.

This type of high-level caliber of principles is what builds real, first-class individuals who are entrusted with great things in life. You can have an expert with technical know-how, but if you can't be trusted at this level in relationships with others, your level of success will be capped and limited.

Chapter 8

Your Home

Often, we have all the tools to be great at our jobs. If we are businessmen, we are good at business plans, making sound choices, and getting the job done. Yet, we rarely sit down and create a business plan or model for our own life. Typically, when we get home from work, we stop applying some of the same sound principles we use at work and wonder why our personal life is so messed up. We become unfocused at home and just want to go on autopilot and do mindless things to disconnect from work.

    I get it! Who wants to come home and do work or be in work mode all over again? No one! But often you speak to coworkers and your boss better than friends and family because, quite frankly, you're comfortable, and you feel they are locked in. They always say we treat the ones we love the most the worst.

Well, it's true, but it's because we have inner struggles that we vent out to those in close proximity. What sucks is that it's not that you don't love or care about them; it's a simple fact of logistics. You've left a hard day at work, and you're mad or frustrated. When you come home, it gets dumped out by default. So, when the big question comes:—"Hey, how was your day?"—if that other person is cheerful and upbeat and you're upset about your day, that question is like a loaded gun. The other person may not know, and you unload and relive that crap, and worse, everyone around—your wife, kids, dog, neighbor—gets to relive the worst part of your day. It now becomes the worst part of their day.

Bottom line: Leave your baggage at the freaking door! Man up to keep the peace and harmony inside your temple, your kingdom, your home. It's a good place to get away from all that negative crap, otherwise, you just brought in a bag of trash and dumped it all over your nice house. If you do this day in and day out, guess what? Your home is now a dumpsite. This doesn't mean you don't want them to ask how your day was, because then you create a silent void. Just say, "Oh, it's work." Why? Because it *is* work. Work ain't always easy, and that's why it's called *work*. I understand that not everyone has this issue, but many people do.

Most people do not have a job they love. The point is, it doesn't matter about the job. What matters is the trash you bring into your home environment. You control that completely. It's a trained behavior you must master, or you run the risk of killing positive energy. Beyond the words, you should also leave negative emotions and body language at the front door. You should transform your state of mind and self before you walk inside.

Clear your thoughts and mind for a few minutes if you need to and focus on what's beautiful and good inside the home. Focus on how you want to protect that space from the outside world. Inside your home is the world you get to control by choice. Most of the time, what got me frustrated at work was one pure evil idiot—a thorn in my side. Instead of identifying these people, I allowed them to control my feelings and emotions, even when I knew they were trash.

The fact that I allowed these people to change my attitude or character was stupid. Then I, in return, acted stupid. It was like a virus, and they had infected me. You can't control other people or most events, but what you can control is your character in all situations, and that yields a better result for you and the people around you. It sounds simple, yet it's hard to master.

Men and women who can master this are successful people in many ways and levels because they don't allow the external factors to affect them. These people can focus on real things. I'd say most people can't master this. They just want to complain about their situation and think that if they can somehow replace that person, things might change. The greatest change to this world we can ever truly make is the change inside ourselves. We must change our own perspective and actions to be the example for others to emulate.

Otherwise, we get billions of disgruntled, negative humans on a shrinking Earth. The kid in the movie *Matrix* said, "It is not the spoon that bends; it is ourselves." I thought, What the heck is he talking about? He's saying the spoon is not what changes; it's you that must change to see the world differently. You can control you, but it's impossible to control the laws of physics. Change your state of mind about what you can do and achieve, and things are possible. Without that, you'll never see real change or your full potential.

"Whoever loves discipline loves knowledge, but whoever hates correction is stupid." (Proverbs 12:1)

Since you are the captain of your own ship, you control the steering. No one's going to steer for you or tell you where to go. Well, actually that's BS; lots of people, groups, and influencers will attempt sway you. Ultimately, when you want to take command of your life, it will be up to you to take over that position. Now it will be your choice on who you allow on your journey, so choose wisely. Taking control, with courage and confidence, is the challenge. As men, we often want to compare and ask other men their thoughts and direction, but no one has to live with your choices other than you.

I find that talking to good men that I admire and respect helps me reveal and pull out the answer I truly seek. If you have friends or family whom you solicit advice from, be careful, because often if you don't follow their advice, they get upset. Be clear that you will consider what they say, but the final choice is yours and yours alone. If they care about you, they want the best for you. Sometimes we must fail and go against sound advice to learn by the actual experience. Personal direct experience has no substitute in life; it's why history does, and always will, repeat itself.

Know that once you've had enough life experiences, you'll wake up to life and realize who you can and can't go to for advice. You'll start to see the clear path and not need anyone's advice anymore. That's when the student of life starts becoming the teacher and understands life's dynamics. This will start to open all the doors you've been searching for. Believing in yourself and your abilities as a mature adult takes a tremendous amount confidence. So, I'm sure you're saying, "How do I get that confidence, and where does it come from?"

The source of and building of that confidence comes when you have failed so much and tried everything you know. When you have exhausted every ounce of yourself and finally try life His way. Yeah, I'm talking about belief in your faith, which is the missing link. He pushed you beyond your limits of what you thought you could do—at the point you are broken and ready to give up. He will show up if you finally take a leap of faith and trust him. What does it say on every piece of American currency? "In God we trust." It's right in front of your face for a reason—not "In God we love," but "In God we trust."

My friend, this is the true breakthrough of this entire book. In the beginning, the formula states that Faith=Success. When you reach adulthood, from codependent to independent, from this world and solely on yourself, you're going to need some help. There is no higher power than the one who created you and this universe. You can give him or her any name you wish: the source, master architect, Buddha, Yahweh, Jesus, Sun, or God. If I can impart anything to you that is most important to your total life success, it will be attributed to your newfound faith.

When I say your faith, I mean your unique and personal relationship with your creator. If you don't have faith in Him, why in the world would He have faith in you to do great things on the planet He created for you to live on? I wouldn't entrust anything important to someone who had all these gifts that I designed and created for them, but who had no faith. The real question is, "Would you?" If you taught your children something special but they abused that gift and used it for themselves and not for loved ones, how would you feel? I only know these things because I am a father myself, just like ABBA, the ancient Aramaic God.

THE LOST ART OF FAITH

When you become a father or mother or caretaker, you start to understand the ways of God—your first father. It's just a huge connect-the-dots puzzle, going backwards from the point you are at now. As you are reading, I am typing, not knowing who will read this book. I had to produce faith by my actions in order for this book to get started.

If you truly want to obtain real inner and outer success, you will have to have belief in your own faith. I do not care to brand any one religion or turn down any religion. Those are all elective tools and resources for something special we have inside of us. That is the seed from your father, and that is the power of God in us. If you don't ever come to realize this gift and this truth, you will not be able to tap into its power. Belief in your faith and connection to your father, God, in this way is the power, the light, and the truth.

Hear this next part: Love is not an emotion. Love is a connection. A connection! The moment you love your father and start that connection, what do you think will happen, and what do you think the possibilities are? Well, if you've lived life on your own terms and by your own ways, how far has that gotten you? Personally, it got me to the top, and because I thought more of myself than God, He showed me very quickly what the good book has to say about that: *"The Lord giveth, and the Lord taketh away."* I was powerless, and I mean powerless—like a single ant versus my own foot.

ERIC DUPRE'

People say to me, "I don't hear or see him". You don't really have to hear or see him, but we all feel the effects of his presence and power. This should be enough to get your attention. Many men have been awakened to his calling. The calling is to be a better man, which in turn makes a man more successful. The good book is nothing more than a mega self-help doctrine of living so we can become successful in all ways of life.

It's also a historical repeat of huge societies that have failed to recognize what I'm telling you and what this book is trying to tell you. If you're dying, do you want a long-term treatment, or do you truly just want a cure or real solution? I'm not interested in money and dragging things out to take your money. So, after you read this book, the only other book I'd advise you to buy is the good book, and most of the time you can get them for free, thanks to The Gideons International.

I can only tell you that the good book saved my life the night my wife told me she was going to leave me. That very night, I checked into a hotel room and turned my phone off. I lay in bed and stared up at the ceiling, saying, "I need a freaking sign from you. I need to see something or know something. Please help me to know." I hoped the TV would come on by itself or the lights would flicker. Absolute silence. No signs. Nothing. All my hope in the world was just about gone.

THE LOST ART OF FAITH

Yeah, I was so driven on emotions that I couldn't see or even think clearly. I was asking Him to do dog tricks to prove Himself to me when He's had nothing to prove to me, just like I have nothing to prove to any other man. We have to show our worth in this world for other men to see and follow.

As I lay there and became calm, my mind gained some clarity and logic. I thought to myself, Let me reach into this top drawer and see if there a Bible. Bingo! Then, I did test him again, and I thought to myself, I'll turn to any one of these twelve hundred pages, and let's see if it speaks to me. I came to page 1,146, which is Ephesians 2:8: *"For by grace you have been saved through faith, and that not of yourselves. It is the gift of God, not of works, lest anyone should boast."*

When I read this, I knew he was speaking directly to me. I was starting to use my common sense and logic, not a stain of an image of Jesus in my sheets . . . which would be very weird. This was just the beginning for me. This was the message that brought me to the door. I was thirty-six at the time. It took me another three years to figure out how to open the door.

Know that you'll make advancements, but you still might not get it, because honestly, you *want* to be ready, but you aren't. You haven't even started to earn it yet. Sorry folks . . . this process takes a lot of effort. Did you think it would be any different than all the other things in life worth having? Make the effort and commitment.

ERIC DUPRE'

I have no clue where you are in your faith or lack of faith. Either way, this book is about the fact that it is real and completely obtainable for your benefit. Like anything in life, it comes down to this: How bad do you want it?

Men have a tendency to be prideful of their own might. One thing men will never obtain through the work they do here on Earth is faith. Doing a bunch of good deeds is good, no doubt, but that's not the result of faith; it's something you choose to do because you want to. Some people are born with such faith, and some lose their faith, and some never obtain it. Again, this is my story about my faith and how I converted my mind to understand how it translates to a better way of life that creates a better world.

Wherever you draw inspiration from in your walk-through, use it to its fullest to help support your faith. I am all for support and do not judge any man for the sources he uses, as that is not my place. I'm a man who greatly loves this world, this planet, and all the things in it. We are all different; we are all unique and beautiful in our own ways. I honestly don't want to live in a boring world that just conforms to my wishes, I like a little uniqueness. The key is you have to know how to fight and choose your battles, and how to walk right through them without blinking. You have real things to accomplish without having to stop for the petty complications and distractions.

These distractions are the devil's way of delaying you from obtaining real progress. I mean, that's his job, folks. He's designed to do his job well, and he's been doing it for a long, long time. He may just be a necessary evil, so let's make sure we identify him and his role in keeping your life screwed up. We can use evil versus good, or negative versus positive, as long as we are talking about forces we know are real. This will prevent us from overcoming fears and obstacles to reach our best self so we can be happy and satisfied.

"For what is a man profited, if he shall gain the whole world and lose his own soul?" (Matthew 16:26)

You don't have to sell yourself, your morals, or principles to become successful. If you do, rest assured you'll feel it someday, and it's not a place you want to be. To be honest with you, I know it won't last. Shady stuff catches up fast, and in the end, your progress is for nothing. This is not the way to obtain life's success; it just leads to a dead-end road.

Chapter 9

Know Thyself & Control Thyself

The art of mastering self-control is critical. If you have bad thoughts, they will become what you do and say; that's psychology and science 101. The positive thoughts you have force the mind to only consider those thoughts. This is the trick of hypnosis. If a hypnotist can get you in a state of clarity, they can rewire your thinking patterns and behavior. The thing is, you can do it yourself. Just like anything, it takes practice and it takes knowing what you're doing and why.

If you have too many uncontrolled or racing thoughts, it can be hard to hack your brain. If you list out your bad thoughts and issues, you then need to put them to rest and realize that those thoughts no longer serve a purpose in your mind. You need to replace them. This is a huge step in the right direction. Thoughts of work failures, relationships, deaths of loved ones, and bad childhoods get jammed in there. Things that cause pain will cause emotional distress, or cause you to think about that pain when you're faced with the situation again. Anything that's not serving you for a better future needs to go. A better way to look at it is that you need to make your peace about the past so you can move forward.

So, here's how to connect the dots. Something heavy on your heart will constantly be on your mind, and if it's something beyond your control, then it becomes frustrating, causing your emotions to rise. When your emotions rise, they overtake your logic. When your logic is overtaken, you act stupid or illogical, as Spock would tell you, and he'd be right.

So, here's where the secret of faith comes in to play. When one prays over a hard situation, it's a form of meditation that slows your mind and allows your logic to catch up to your emotional distress. Meditation allows you to try to obtain clarity when needed. Keeping calm always allows you to perform better mentally, thus also physically. This is also part of psychology and the science of the body.

When you realize how many choices are not fatal, and how it's not the end of the world, you start to calm down and make better choices without fear of the results. If you learn how to sense and feel yourself and your own emotions, you'll see the pattern of events that you can begin to take control over. So, if you know you have to meet a pissed-off client about a job issue, know that if it gets out of hand and they start yelling at you, no problem, you have already imagined the worst. Tell yourself that you aren't going to react foolishly ahead of time, no matter what, and keep that promise to yourself.

If they start yelling about something, think about your heart rate, as most of the time, if you fear these situations, your heart rate goes up. This is the first sign of anxiety. You'll feel a rush come over you like stress, and then it's a small panic attack. Yes, when your emotions overwhelm you, mentally and physically, you panic. So, in a panic you react, and if you're in a hostile environment, you might attack back or shut down.

This is a very normal reaction. Very few humans can stay calm and collected when being attacked. However, if you are calm under attack, you can remain focused without attacking back. Better yet, you can attack, but you'll know you're in control and how to fight back the right way. The right way is to use your newfound inner strength to stay calm and disarm the confrontation by not making it worse. If you can use this skill and train your mind and body not to react under harsh life conditions, you can start to control life's various situations, one by one, with positive empowerment. I'd rather make peace and have good relationships than fight folks, which is one way to becoming successful. Conflict resolution skills.

THE LOST ART OF FAITH

Learning to work with people, and I mean all people, is a leadership skill. But what I just shared with you is an interesting breakdown that I see all the time: folks allow others to mentally control them and change their mood and behavior. When you have great self-control and you see the positive results of how you've handled difficult situations, you'll gain confidence, and you will most likely produce the best outcome—not the perfect or preferred, but the best. When you chain-link together lots of good choices based on your ability to control yourself, any bad that may have happened from those events—thus the karma effect—will return positivity back to you. If you make bad choices, then surely you'll get the opposite effect.

This doesn't mean that bad things can't or won't happen to you, assuredly they will, but you will have the power to not make them worse. When we make something worse, it just takes that much longer to heal. If you can heal faster, you can learn quicker, as life is just a bunch of failures waiting to happen for you. Yes . . *for* you, not *to* you.

I wrote this for my kids: If something happens and it's good, it's a blessing. If it's bad, then it's just a lesson. If you don't learn from the lesson, then you will fail the next time that test presents itself. The faster you learn this lesson, the quicker you can see the opportunity to work on something you're weak at or don't often see. It's like tripping over a curb after the third or fourth time. You learn to avoid it and/or look out for it.

So back on the topic of hacking the mind by renewing it. Your brain is your strongest tool and resource that you have on planet Earth. The human brain is an organic supercomputer that can figure out so many things, it's beyond comprehension for most. I've forced my brain to do things I never thought it could possibly figure out, so it's like asking myself to write a new computer code for something I know nothing about. What's crazy is that the brain can, and you can learn to teach yourself. All brains are made of the same organic flesh material and function on the same principles as all other human brains. So why in the world are some people smarter or better than others? It boils down to what you're willing to believe and accept for yourself.

Am I saying that if I believe I can do something, I can? Yes! 1000%! It's been proven year after year after year. Humans have done things people said would never be possible, and we did, and we did, and we did, and we did some more. Now that's the power of faith and believing in something unseen and a greater force beyond yourself, as we surely didn't create all this, but we can create damn near anything we put our minds to. This is a fact, and it is truly mind over matter.

The mind can control matter because the brain controls all the organic matter in your body and tells every cell what to do—consciously and subconsciously. If you can dream it or think it, then it can be done. It all starts with a vision, and if you could tap into your fourth-grade dreamer self, at some point, you believed all this was true. But over time, in a conformed society, we tend to follow the masses and what seems to be right based on comfort, normalcy, and ease. No great person did anything based on what others thought, and definitely not based on comfort. So, what we really are talking about here is how to freaking get over stuff that freaks us out, creates fears, and/or creates doubt. Once you face this situation, your emotions and logic have to be jailbroken to work as one. If you don't believe me, ask anyone you know who's done something extraordinary that was unlike anyone had done before them.

Again, this is where great faith comes in, and faith doesn't mean you have it all figured out; it's actually the opposite. You have some of it figured out, but you have enough confidence to get through any situation you really want badly enough in this world. And who can stop you? Just you! For proof, just look at what so many people who come from nothing have been able to accomplish in life. Some people ruled countries, designed the atomic bomb, invented computers and the internet. Some people went to space. Dude! The one thing these people have in common is that they had great faith in something, and once they locked in on that "something," they then had unstoppable faith in themselves.

Now I should forewarn you at this point that with such great confidence and power, many are not prepared for the success, power, and control—or the fact that the success ends at some point. Most do not consider the end or that the end might not be what they had planned, which is why the good book prepares you for that time, as well. Gaining success is only part of the battle; the other half is maintaining success. You want quick success, but when it lands on top of your head and you didn't plan or consider all this success you desired, it overwhelms you. Then what do you do? I'd say once you know what you want do in life, your faith will carry your through the hard parts so you can focus without so much fear of the unknown.

There is a saying that timing is everything, and biblically it's written out that God's timing is not always *our* timing. We often hear people say that the stars need to be aligned. Lots of things need to be right for sustainable success and the management that you will require to be calm and patient. I know you've heard patience is a virtue, so it will not be any different for us. If you're reading this to correct things that might not be 100%, that's great, because having some errors forces people to correct the speaker, which just means they are actually paying attention to the material.

THE LOST ART OF FAITH

I've done this intentionally in some of my speaking engagements so that when they point it out, I can speak about that topic more in depth. I also like folks to know that I'm not perfect, nor do I ever claim to be, which is part of my message. Practice doesn't make perfect; it makes better. Perfection is only measured to a level of degree we accept as a standard that was set by someone else at some point in time. Striving for perfection is the goal of mastery, but that measurement is often not obtainable until your life's work is complete, and often that extends beyond death, based on what you left behind.

"Success is not final, failure is not fatal: it is the courage to continue that counts." —Winston Churchill

Chapter 10

Needs Versus Wants

To have a successful life, you need to understand what you truly need versus what you want. Today's current society thinks we need everything. When it comes to those expectations, we set ourselves up for failure. If everything is a need and you become needy or dependent on things for happiness, you're addicted to things. These addictions and distractions consume us, making it hard to focus and concentrate on what our true priorities are. So, back to the KISS method. Less is more, because with less we can truly appreciate what we have and it gets the real attention that it deserves.

Needs are what you must have to survive in life. *Wants* are things you don't need emotionally, but you can build a dependency on them until those wants feel like needs. This happens in the multi-billion-dollar industries in America. We are fighting like hell to not get addicted to foods, TV shows, video games, social media, and so forth. The way these things are marketed is mentally unhealthy for us as a society, and for our kids' future, because left unchecked, it will just get worse. These industries do not want you to save money; they want you to spend it. If you invested your money versus acquired wealth, that wouldn't sit too well with the folks who run this joint. Most of our hard-earned money is not invested into our kids' future; it's invested in the wealthy's future and their kids.

I'm not saying not to do anything and not to buy stuff. What I'm saying is, look at the bigger picture and find some balance. The trend in America is to buy more stuff. It's sad because we have way less human interaction than ever before, and people are lonely and unhappy being lonely. Our capitalistic superpowers are well aware of this trend, and they exploit it to sell and make as much money as humanly possible.

To help open others' eyes to these dynamics is part of living a successful life—to help folks see something they might not see and how it's working against them and is counterproductive to their goals. We want a secure future for ourselves and our children, but when we have so many forces working against us, it becomes difficult to see the light at the end of the tunnel and not just follow everyone. Don't deprive yourself; find balance, and be disciplined.

Controlling our desires falls in this section because often our desires are just excessive wants. When we want bigger things in life, like a wife, home, and kids, we must be careful. To get the things you seek will require making money to provide for all these things. There are also personal wants you naturally would like for yourself, as well, which also require money. Thus, the pitfall of money becomes a primary focus. These desires often distract us from the priorities of God and family first. If you can't control your desires on a lower level, then you will surely struggle at a higher one.

When we decide to cross over to this stage of life, things get very deep. Once you have clawed your way to dependence, you will then want to make a commitment to struggle with another human because you are in love. If this is true love, it has tons of power; but that power in a marriage often dies down over time because marriage isn't easy. In fact, it's a lot of effort if you want to have a good marriage—just like a good but difficult job that rewards you.

We amass more debt in marriage—student loans, cars, houses, credit cards—and then we have as many kids as we like or can afford, and the cycle starts all over again. To break bad cycles or behavior takes a lot of discipline in our faith because all we want is to maintain happiness. Yet all of the things discussed above cause stress, and you have discord and fighting as an effect of the stress, which often leads to unhappiness, which can lead to depression and divorce. Millions of people, however, don't get depressed or freak out or get divorced. They quite possibly have the same issues, yet they are happy. These folks live in their faith and align their family with that faith and act accordingly.

Those happier families often produce more at higher levels. Not because they go to church every Sunday, not because they read the good book every night, but because someone in the home lives in faith, guided by our creator, and gives instruction to a true, loving family. The family follows the leader's example. When you have two married people and the faith isn't aligned, or one parent truly doesn't have their own faith, it will be a massive struggle. When the two actually share their faith, then you have an almost indestructible household.

How do I know this? I lived in this household, but it was *I* who didn't have the faith when my wife did. I questioned her almost daily on her faith, which was exhausting and draining. At the time, I didn't see the light. I didn't understand the how or the why. I became codependent on her for strength and answers for my own messes, but when she needed strength and support, since I had no real faith, I honestly had nothing to offer her in hard times. I'm not a liar and never have been, so when she wanted me to tell her and the kids everything would be okay, I couldn't because I couldn't see how it would be okay because I had no real faith.

One of the worst feelings in the world is to have your wife crying on the ground, and not being able to tell her what she needs to hear because you are a weak man of little faith. I personally don't want any man to ever feel that kind of pain and suffering, to see what he loves so much in pain, and can't say or doing anything because he's simply not prepared for life. We spend so much time in education. I took thirteen years of public and two years of technical school, yet I still didn't know what to do.

When you take God and faith out of teaching a love-based, living doctrine, this is what you get: Success in everything except for what matters most in life, people, and relationship values. Most might say that's supposed to take place at home, and to those lucky persons, I say that you didn't grow up in the 50–60% of broken homes in America. I'm sorry it's this way, but that's why I'm writing this book: to save one kid, one parent, one family, one life that could change the course of history or their life someday by learning from my failures and the lessons I've learned.

We need to teach our youth more faith-based principles. We need more people to be okay with what I'm saying so we can change our society's fundamental breakdown before it's too late. We need a collective effort to teach things like "*love your neighbor as yourself*" and "*honor your parents.*"

Chapter 11

Struggling Through Any Process: "No Pain, No Gain"

I'm sure you've heard the expression, "If it was easy, everyone would do it." Well, when something is hard to obtain, you know you'll be in rare company, as lots of folks give up when things get hard. When you realize that's part of the gift of struggling, you'll also realize it's a good thing.

When you want to accomplish something worthwhile, you really have to dig in, put effort into it, and earn it. The greater the glory, the greater the effort. Why do you think people break down in tears of joy when they win a championship? Because of all the hard work. More so, because of the pain and suffering it cost them, and the things they probably had to give up, while not knowing if they'd ever be champions. They may have failed over and over and thought they might never be able to taste that glory. But when you finally buy in to the system and go all in—mind, body, and spirit—you break through that freaking wall. The feeling is so great and so well-deserved.

If you want real proof of what I'm saying, look at the New England Patriots' head coach, Bill Belichick. He gets the most out of players when they arrive. How and why? I'll tell you his secret, and I've never even met him; I've only observed his success and listened to what the players have to say about him. He gets the most out of them because they have been failures and overlooked by everyone else. They know it, and Bill knows it. So, with that you ask them: Do you want to keep being a failure like *they* think you are, or do you want to be a champion and prove them wrong? This is where the motivation and fire starts.

When you look a human in the eye and ask them these questions, do you know what you can do with hungry, motivated, passionate humans that listen? What you get is a team of highly-driven individuals that would battle through Hell for each other, and this, my friend, produces champion teams. But you also don't get that until the individual commits to believing in the system, which takes absolute trust, and then it takes faith. So, again, when we want to talk about faith equaling success, what better example could I give you? Do you see Bill with some kind of giant cross on his neck? Nope! When you understand the power of faith, you don't boast about it; you let your actions do all the talking for you. His actions tell me without a doubt, this man has learned from other men how to harness and sustain power.

Power, under control, is called *meekness*, and I've not seen many men under stressful conditions hold their crap together better than him. He knows when to allow his emotions to come out, which is when the confetti drops—and not a second sooner. Because you never celebrate early when the battle is still being fought. If you know about football, you'll know what I mean. The Atlanta Falcons' owner made this mistake years ago in the Super Bowl. When I saw him come to the sideline, I knew Bill Belichick used that to fire up his troops. I'm sure he said something like, "Men, they think you're done and dead, but let's show them with everything we got left in us, and let's fight our way back into this thing." Knowing how loyal and how much these men believe in their coach, I'm pretty sure they fought like no one's business to win. And they did win.

Now, do you wanna keep doing what you're doing the way you're doing it, or do you want to try something new that might be temporarily uncomfortable but could be a game changer, where you truly earn and get the total life success you've been thirsting for? The commitment costs you zero dollars. What plan on the market today to finding ultimate success costs you zero dollars? The peace, love, joy, and success you are looking for has always been so close to you. Fear of what others might think or say is nothing. Do you truly put God first in all things you do, or do you even consider God in the things you do? To pause when you need to make decisions that are important and consider what is right leads to one thing: righteousness.

There is always a right and wrong, but we often sell ourselves on wrong because it's easy. Easy and wrong just become a bad habit or bad program in your mind. We sell ourselves on, "Well, it's not that bad," or, "Buddy is a good guy, and *he* does it." The bottom line is, inside you, and inside the rest of us, is a little voice that knows it just ain't right. But we bypass that discernment and make bad choices. When you add up tiny bad choices over long periods of time, what do you think you get? Yeah, you get a truckload of bad choices that amount to a lot, but once little bad choices become a comfortable habit, bigger and bigger bad choices occur. It's like a sickness or computer virus that infects you and highjacks you over time.

Time is very important to this equation, which is why I've written this book. The more time you are afforded to live a successful life of peace, love, and joy in this world, the more you will have a profound effect on those around you. When this chain reaction occurs, it could be the atomic bomb we need to see real change. Real knowledge, wisdom, and intelligence are only real when something changes on a global scale, but it can be a single individual who sparks this change, which is the most powerful gift God can give a single human. That, my friend, is a miracle, and to be honest, that power lies inside each of us. And this is the greatest secret that can be revealed to mankind.

I can guarantee you that there are no shortcuts to where you need to go, and there is no promise that I can make to you personally. Outside of that, it is fully in your hands. When you start using logic and faith collectively to manage yourself and your life, you'll see great changes. Life happens while we are planning it, but planning forces you to project, think, and prepare for your journey.

At the age of thirty-six, I started to lose everything I loved in this world. That was just three years ago. I lost my wife and two beautiful daughters to a divorce I could not stop. I lost my house, cars, and a lot of money. I lost a place in my own company, and I lost my dog, Tyler. I lost my drive, my motivation, my mind, and at one point, I lost my will to live in the pain and the suffering that goes with losing what you love the most. I begged and begged God to spare me from the pain and torture. My heart was flooded with hate, anger, and raw fury. All these things led to a path of destruction and to a dead-end.

The logical part of my brain said, "You don't have crap left other than your faith. Don't lose hope in the one last thing keeping you afloat." So, I didn't. Not only did I not lose hope, I aimed my ship straight toward Him as my only course and purpose in life. If this good book was so good, I was all in, because I honestly had nothing left. I bought into God's system like a Bill Belichick system. I wanted God to coach me, and I wanted to finally start winning at life. I was tired of the one-step-forward and two-steps-back dance. I wanted my cake, and I wanted to enjoy it as well. Now, I never had a big moment, but I had a bunch of solid moments in this process, and I knew and felt that I was on the right track.

    There is a process taught in elementary school called *the scientific method*. You start with a problem, you formulate a hypothesis of what you think is the correct answer, and then you test it out. If it doesn't work, you can cross it off the list and keep experimenting while learning from your previous experiment. You do this until you start seeing results that appear to solve the problem. As a man, what faith has taught me is that I create a lot of my own problems, so part of the solution is mostly in my own hands. The Bible states that with enough faith, a man could move a mountain. Well, if we don't *create* our own mountains, we don't have to move them, which is a lot less work and seems more logical.

    Once you have the gift of faith and accept it as part of yourself, you can be in traffic and focus on a small patch of green grass or the sky, versus building up frustration and anxiety about the traffic that you cannot control. This sounds so simple, yet it's something millions of people struggle with every day. Two things can't occupy the same space, so if you have the choice in any situation—to have a good thought or a bad thought—you can choose to replace one with the other. If you allow a bad thought to sit in the center of your mind—the most powerful thing on planet Earth and the most powerful tool you have—what do you think is going to happen?

We will all have bad thoughts enter our minds, but how fast we rid our minds of those things and replace them with better thoughts will form strong, positive habits. This will change how you see and react to things in this world, or better yet, you will no longer have an urge to react in haste. You become a James Dean who's always cool, calm, and collected. Chicks dig that guy, and so do other men. We all want that kind of swagger. This is a mastery of self-control that brings forth a personal confidence.

Dale Carnegie writes about handling yourself with class. After reading many self-help books, I'll let you in on a little secret I've learned: The root that all these books center around is the core principle of how to conduct yourself in society when everyone's acting like a damn fool. The source of these books is the Bible through a different perspective. Make no mistake—when it comes to living a righteous, successful life, it requires more than just a book. It first starts deep inside you, as a want to change your patterns and yield a better output than what you've been getting. The friends and family you have around you are also part of this because everything is centered around relationships, otherwise we'd have no clue if we were acting like a man or animal. We need a comparison and/or confirmation from trusted individuals.

We live in an adult world and are perceived to have matured from child to adult. Spiritual maturity is a whole other ball game. Once you can act like an upright, mature adult, and once you have found your faith and matured in it and aligned the two, then you start to see the power of yourself come to life. To keep our bodies alive, to repeat the tasks we did the day before, over and over, takes little effort. To transform that body into a spiritual being is a transformation I believe can take a man from average to something special. If you can make the transformation happen, you will feel it inside of you, and other people around you will also take notice.

I've seen this transformation take place first-hand in other men. It's truly a game changer, and I think anytime someone mentions that something is a game changer, we want a piece of it. Life is a game that we can either choose to play or sit on the sidelines. Many will play, but few will change the game. My hope and dream from this book is to open up your heart and mind to find the game changer in you, because I want you to release your best upon this, and your, world. I want one dude to walk up to me and say, "Eric, your book really opened my eyes up and helped me achieve so much more in life than I could have ever imagined."

ERIC DUPRE'

I was told something simple: Just do your best. That's all the guidance I was truly given, and I was like, no crap! The thing is, that person couldn't tell me more because that's all they knew to say. But in truth, our best is only what we believe ourselves, and our beliefs are limited by what we think.

God helped me find my best by crushing me and hurting me, or allowing me to fail and fail and fail to the point where I was lost. It sounds horrible, and believe these words—I can't even begin to articulate the hell and torture I endured. But finally, I busted out of that jail of Hell. I learned to stop using my own limited abilities and tiny man-brain, and to allow my true beliefs in my God to do what He says He can do when we choose to believe in Him by our true absolute faith in Him. When I committed to that, He busted me out of my own jail of Hell on Earth.

Finally, I slowed my brain and thinking down. When your brain runs like a bullet-train, you have racing thoughts, which lead to out-of-control worries. Out-of-control worries lead to mental stress, which lead to anxiety, and anxiety to panic attacks. When you panic out of fear of an event that hasn't happened yet, you've self-destructed. Folks end up getting scared, which causes another panic attack, and they can't get out of their nightmare. It's also known as PTSD caused by traumatic events.

If you can stop the first domino from falling, none of the rest will fall. I want you to really, really hear this: If you stop the first domino, the rest simply cannot fall. You have to figure out what triggers your anxiety, so once you know what it is and when it's coming, you can prepare to shut it down ahead of time. This takes practice, but we'll get plenty of that practice in life. When we take medications to prevent or minimize the effects of anxiety, we can also alter other mental aspects of our focus and clarity. Do what you must do, but know if you understand how something works, you can start to take control over it before it takes control of you. The Bible talks about the renewal of your mind, which to me means taking back control of your mind.

There's something bigger to consider in all of this if you believe in an afterlife—or simply, Heaven. Everything I'm talking about in this book will also guide you toward a successful worldly life, but more importantly, it will guide you toward the gates of Heaven. We are all going die, you know that, so if there is an afterlife and necessary steps to be taken to prepare for that final destination as the ultimate success, you really need to heed this message I bring.

Let's pretend you get all the riches you ever wanted, and then you die. What the hell? That's it? No, no way is that it. There is a place you will go that is so far beyond your imagination, it is the true treasure you and I seek. There is nothing on this Earth that we could ever obtain that would quench that ultimate knowledge and euphoric love. If you had an infinite state of pure euphoric love, what price would you pay for that? Anything and everything we have! The beauty of this book and message that I bring is that you can find your peace and fulfillment here on Earth while you wait for your time to *not die*, but to pass into a realm of euphoric love forever and reunite with everything you ever loved.

What if I'm wrong? If I'm wrong and you changed to be a better man, husband, father, worker, friend, or businessman, and you lived a better, righteous life, would you be mad at me? I highly doubt this single book will make a real difference when the other book is resting in billions of homes right now. I'm not the apostle Paul, I'm not the Pope, I'm not the Dalai Lama, or Morgan Freeman. I'm just Eric Dupre'. The only thing I have in common that might give me a chance to broadcast this message is I know I have the same kind of faith in love that these men have for this world, and I'm willing to face this entire world head-on to defend that gift at my own expense and ridicule. The only thing I ask of you is to consider what I'm saying and see what fits or sticks for you. I've asked for no promise, no joining of any group, and no action towards anyone else but yourself, by your own free will. I want to leave behind something beneficial to you from my personal experience, because that is truly the greatest gift I could give. If this book helps just one person, we moved a mountain . . . or helped not to create one.

Faith helps keep our mental state strong, which is similar to building up a good immune system for your body.

Just as your body learns how to fight off diseases and viruses, so must we learn how to do the same mentally. We have all heard the term *manifestation*, which is when a thought, idea, or theory becomes an action. A thought is just a thought until it becomes observed by the world. That's when it becomes real. And it all starts with a tiny thought or vision of what can or could be. The generation of good, positive thoughts is something within our control, so we can flood our mental state with those thoughts and push out or replace bad thoughts.

The Power of Positive Thinking by Norman Vincent Peale, is a great book, published in the fifties, that hammers home this concept like no other. It was read by some of the most successful people around the world and is another dot in the connect-the-dots process of renewing yourself from the inside out by way of changing your way of thinking. Positive thinking is the key to positive outcomes, as well as healing negative ailments like depression.

We have our conscious and subconscious. The conscious is the part of our thoughts we are aware of and can control, for the most part. Our subconscious is the deeper part that runs our heart, breathing, blinking, etc., based on what it needs. Now, there are years of events recorded in your subconscious' computer database that we are often unaware of until we want to be. We can force our minds to think and recall many things, but many times, your body knows you better than you do and wants to protect you from hurting yourself; that includes your mind.

It can force you to block out something or cause you to reject that information because it may be painful to deal with. But to overcome something in life, we must face these fears and hard truths to get past something that blocks us from doing or becoming who we want to be in life. Again, I know this information is deep for most of us, but with faith, you can overcome some of your biggest fears in life. Faith *starts* with a belief but never *becomes* faith until your actions match your beliefs. Then and only then can we start to see the power of faith. This is something that takes a lot of mental discipline and a real desire, just like when you wanted a car, or house, or degree, or girlfriend, or video game, or first place. It doesn't matter what we want as long as it's a priority, and we'll automatically think about it, talk about it, dream about it, and if we take real steps of action to support it, it will happen. Once you see this concept come to life and you test it out, or better yet, already know it to be true, it becomes a matter of test driving it until you see it and truly believe it as fact.

If you have a common vision with other individuals, this can and will help advance your goal. You are sharing something that creates this "vibe" or feeling of comfort, and they get you. When external factors aren't apparent, it's hard to trust that feeling because humans are hardwired and designed to trust so much through sight. In my opinion, this is why faith is such a hard concept.

As adults, we often need to seek the proof that something is real, but just because we can't see something doesn't mean it isn't there. Radio waves carry signals so you can jam out in the car on the way to work. Can you see the music floating in the air on the way to your antenna? No! But do you have faith that it will work when you get in the car and turn it on? Yes! Do you know how it works? No! But you believe in it anyway, and it works. The fact that it works is what we love about it. God works in mysterious ways, but the key word in that phrase is *works*. Again, we don't fully understand how He works, but that's the part of faith that is also key. We know how we work as humans, and if we hack into ourselves and tap into the power of faith, placing it in our conscious and subconscious as a good doctrine of living and as the foundational principles of living good, it will be manifested from these actions.

Good manifests into success, as bad things are not sustainable. It's easier to change yourself than it is to change the world, but if you change yourself, you *can* change your world. Michael Jackson had a powerful, global hit song called "Man in the Mirror." When messages are powerful, we should pay attention. The song was designed to have a catchy hip-hop beat to it because he wanted as many people to not only hear it, but to also receive the message. If you look at some of the most successful artists, movies, and sports stories, the messages of faith and the foundational principles faith is based on are usually part of that story. We all have our own story as well, and my hope is that after you read this book, you'll start to shape your own story for the better. It's my hope to awaken you with some real tools to help you achieve real, fulfilled success, and so you can help make this world a better place.

Chapter 12

Key Ingredients: Mind, Body, Spirit

When one mixes the key ingredients/elements with the right amounts together, you can create just about anything you desire or will intentionally. You must come to realize you are the master chief of your own mind, body, and spirit and ultimately the final product of your own life. The power of faith requires the proper portion and mixture over time, just like a cake. You find this in chemistry, science, nature, baking, and in faith. When all three elements of mind, body, and spirit are brought together in peace and with purpose, by your own choice, you will see your life change forever. Each element serves a specific function and when they are all working collectively for what you desire, you will be on fire and you will feel it and know it.

ERIC DUPRE'

The body is this machine in which, to run efficiently, you need to balance and harmonize these three things. The chemicals your body produces or doesn't produce can greatly alter and effect your mind, emotions, and health of all three elements. When one of more of these gets out of line, your entire being can be way off. When I work out, I notice a huge improvement of mental strength. It has a lot to do with the blood flow and oxygen carried to feed your body. Blood flow to the brain and extra oxygen always helps your brain perform better as without it you start to shut down.

Your emotional state has a lot to do with chemicals produced in the body. If you look at today's work environment, we have so much machine automation that humans are doing less and less physical activity than at any point in history, yet our diets are the same if not worse for calorie intake because the food we love and crave create dopamine which makes it addictive. We are slammed with dopamine which is a chemical that triggers motivational reward. It can make you feel happy or sad and can make you feel very erratic because your body's chemistry wants that craving very bad. This can include, and not limited to, sex, food, drugs, alcohol, and even likes or dislikes from Facebook. Crazy stuff!

The retail world wants you crave things, but again everything in moderation. Take your mind, body, and spirit back and gain control by slowly lessening your needs for things, there is much you can do to break yourself of dependency. At this point, I honestly think adults need a month-long detox, which isn't going happen, but if you study other countries, you see that they understand this balance and protect their people from ingesting too many chemicals.

If you haven't noticed, so many things of this world as we know it are working against the average Joe, to farm out people that can be controlled through a structured system that works against you. Once you start to realize that these principles aren't really what you've signed up for, you'll really holistically start looking at basing your life around solid doctrine principles that are here to help you, even when there are many complex variables working against you. It goes back to the basic, fundamental principles of the good book. How these principles, applied in your life, will be part of your own free will and choice, but again, this is a connect-the-dots game. You need to identify a pattern that is or isn't working for you. If all these things are working for you then great don't change a thing, but if it ain't, you need to consider this information for your own benefit.

2 Timothy 3:16
All scripture is given by inspiration of God, and is profitable for doctrine, for reproof, correction, for instruction in righteousness.

ERIC DUPRE'

There's a reason they call it the "good book", it's the best written, self-help guide to total and complete success of life. There is a clear pattern of the good things it speaks of, when you mirror that of people who actually live it out by actions. Most people of great faith just know it works and stick to the format because, it works, and they don't care how, it just does. More than likely that behavior was passed down as a gift, from generation to generation, but who knows? I'm telling you the more aligned we are with this book the more positive results we will benefit in all aspects of life collectively. I'm not here to covert you to anything, I'm here to give and be an example of it works. I'm not telling anyone to go to any particular place of faith. Do I have my own preferences? Of course, I do, and my faith is completely unique to me. Just like a relationship we share with other people, it's unique between the two individuals.

Where I'm at in my process of faith is also different. Which is why respecting someone's walk in faith is very important because we aren't always at the same place, at the same time. But if we share a common overall vision our target is the same. If our target is the same our alignment at some point shall fall into place as well in due time.

Keep feeding yourself healthy things so you can produce good fruits for the world to feed off of.

Chapter 13

Superhuman Behavior/Breaking Yourself

To be supernatural is to be unnatural. Humans are animals, and we have built-in animal instincts and triggers. It's human nature. When you break yourself and change your natural tendencies, you're taking unnatural things under your control. This is truly supernatural. When you want to react out of primal animal instinct, yet you remain calm and focused and you do what's right despite certain conditions, that is remarkable. A man who has this control can often control his environment—not the other way around. We talk about man being a product of our environment. Well, that all depends. If you hated that environment and realize there's a better environment, you can obtain it. If you want it, go get it.

Behavior is a habitual reaction we absolutely control. Our reactions are typically based on the emotional drivers inside of us. The seven universal emotions are:

1. Anger
2. Fear
3. Disgust
4. Happiness
5. Sadness
6. Surprise/Anticipation
7. Trust/Distrust

Having complete mastery and control over your emotions is what these mega pastors nationwide are speaking about—being supernatural based on biblical teaching. Of the seven emotions listed, only two are deemed good, and the others are bad. This means you have to work a lot harder to maintain your cool, as the odds are stacked against you until you learn how to harness the power of your faith. When we jump back and forth between the five negative emotions is when the wheels really come off the bus. This book is just a quick start guide to get you to see how all this works for or against you.

THE LOST ART OF FAITH

Having a planet full of angry and frustrated humans is not good for me, my kids, or anyone. At the end of the day, I need y'all locked in, engaged, and wanting to read more so you soak up the good stuff and start planning your life-changing attack to success. In thirty-six intense, hardcore months, I spent thousands of hours seeking, reading, trying, praying, counseling, going to men's groups, and having lunches with pastors. You name it, I've done it. I even met Joel Osteen during the process of this book. I've spent the time and money to hack deep into this revelation about solving for life's success by developing faith and a way of life based on the presented information.

Of all of these emotions, fear is by far the worst. Fear is flat out slavery, and you are a slave to it. If I had to call the devil another name, it would just be *fear*.

"Even though I walk through the valley of the shadow of death, I will fear no evil: for thou art with me; thy rod and thy staff, they comfort me." Psalm 23:4

The greatest power of true, unshakeable faith is truly amazing when a man stops fearing things of this world. Know that your God, who created all, will do with you as He pleases. You can then walk with peace knowing that if you live by His good doctrine, He'll have your back all the way. Not many men can cross this threshold, as they fear dying, losing loved ones, or losing a job or house. Guess what? We're all going to lose it all in the end, so don't fear it. That will only make life worse for you. Have you ever wondered why some dudes don't get rattled by anything? I'm one of those guys for two reasons: I had to confront all my worst fears in thirty-six months, and I'm not afraid of death because to me, it's *not* death; it's an afterlife.

Facing your worst fears frees your mind so you can find some peace. Sometimes you have to go through your own hell on Earth to truly break your fears so you can overcome and be more in the future. If not, you will surely be enslaved to those fears the rest of your time. Realize that God will not let you die until He's ready for you, and nothing on Earth can prevent or speed up that moment. Since the one true creator created all, he also *controls* all, and no power in Heaven or on Earth can change that.

What's also helped me to fight fear is that part of the Bible that talks about sons of men, and another part that talks about sons of God. Since we are all created by God, we have a piece of Him as part of our DNA code. I feel that it's not triggered until you fully accept this through your complete faith in Him. We are all children of God. Think about this. Did you choose your parents, place, and time you were born? Nope. Neither did I. One could conclude that randomly we could be any other person ever born on this planet. Knowing that should wake you up to how you would treat a different version of yourself born into a different set of life circumstances.

Behavioral patterns are taught by seeing repetitive behaviors by others, checked habits, and uncontrolled responses due to traumatic mental stress/neuro transmitter malfunction. Either way, this is linked to the domino effect. When X occurs, a person's natural response is what they are programmed and wired to do. Many hard-to-control behaviors come from an emotional overload response. This can be cursing, eating tons of food, buying stuff to feel happy, and so forth. The bulk of this stuff is buried in our subconscious.

We need to find the root cause and the "triggers" that often compel us to react unfavorably or sometimes even uncontrollably. The reason I dig so deep into all of this is that our core taught values, morals, principles, and character as a foundation weren't complete, so these bad programs cause us to fight ourselves, which causes frustration and can hurt relationships. And often, we don't know why it happened or how to fix it. So, when we get a partner and we don't even know we have these issues (because life hasn't gotten complicated or stressful yet), these issues can worsen when you add the cars, house, kids, school, career, love life, time, faith, and so on.

You can probably see why the divorce rate is off the Richter scale. This is a simple pattern and domino effect. When they say we don't want these kinds of teachings in our schools, you then say these kids should get that at home. Well, the fact of the matter is many kids nowadays don't have two parents who understand all this to teach it, and/or they are busy working to keep the roof over the head and food on the table. I was one of those kids. Faith was not a priority in my home by teaching it from parent to child, so I personally know that it left me behind the eight ball, so to speak, on how to use my faith or what it even was. My mom was a hardworking, young, single mother who did the best she could, but that doesn't negate the fact that lack of these taught principles as a lesson never got taught.

If we like the current divorce rates, people-hating, living like angry fools, and little kids getting caught up in all of that, then we can keep it the way it is. If we don't like the way society looks, then we need some change and to do a better job making people feel comfortable about faith.

Dr. Martin Luther King would have loved to see this message as a man of faith, and as a doctor, because he would have loved the science, psychology, theology, and science behind the total message. I have a shared dream like Dr. King, as well. It is that we change our behavior patterns and shift from hate to love through understanding and compassion. When people are mentally hurting and sick, we must help them, not abandon them and cast them out as damaged goods. Instead of bitching about all this to no one on Facebook, I'm writing a book and will do my best to find solutions for a failing humanity that so desperately needs help. I have two young daughters who need a better looking future, and as a father, this is my obligation and duty. Like Forrest Gump would say, "That's all I have to say about that!"

Chapter 14

Spiritual Realm 3rd Dimension

It may be taboo to openly talk about spiritual realms or other dimensions, but it's 2019, and if you don't think that exists, you're very late to the party. If you've read this far, you probably anticipated this discussion, as we've used the word *spirit* dozens of times.

When we discuss *faith*, we often talk about Heaven and Earth as two difference places: Earth comprised of space, time, and matter; and Heaven, which does not encompass those same elements. If we are discussing angels, demons, and a spiritual realm outside of our six senses, this would be a place between Heaven and Earth—a third dimension. Many faiths believe in this dimension as a place where spiritual warfare takes place.

THE LOST ART OF FAITH

On Earth, we typically observe that the mind and body operate normally, but the spirit is a unique animal because it doesn't exist in the same plane. It falls partly in you, and the other part is in the spiritual realm. Just like your brain and body, it has many components. Over time, what you feed your body and brain becomes part of what you feed your spirit. Various energy fields from the environment can produce or reduce your power of spirit. When you hear "We're on the same wave length," or "I like that vibe," these are signs that you're feeling something beyond your five senses. It's a sixth sense. When you feel something is wrong or bad, it's a feeling from your spirit. Knowing what is right and wrong, without proof, is discernment—a feeling from the spirit. The clearer you are in your faith, the more it allows your inner spiritual power to guide you. It's the "gut" feeling; a combination of unseen energy fields as well as millions of events registered in your supercomputer database called the *subconscious*.

When the two—discernment and natural thinking—are aligned and functioning, they link to help you make good decisions. Some people believe spirits, vibes, and energy are a joke, but energy floating in the air is just like lightning streaking across the sky. It's not hard to start to see that humans who built radio towers, satellites, and Wi-Fi mirrored this in a vision from the human mind and made it a reality.

So, yeah, the human mind and body are the best, most powerful machines and computers on Earth, and we are way more sophisticated than anyone can ever comprehended. The closer you start to align your mind with this reality, you'll realize that many things are based off of the same principles mirrored in humans, which are created in God's image. The image is the linking of The God Code in all things. I'm giving you a snapshot of deeply linked things that are inside of all of us. If you wish to further explore these things I'm sharing, you'll find tons of supporting information. But until you grasp the source of my information—which comes from the Bible—as the ultimate supporting document that truly connects the dots of your connection back to your creator, by faith, you can't have a relationship with Him because you don't believe. If you don't believe by choice, that's your free will and pride or self-manifested ego. I firmly believe that if you don't believe in anything, you'll wish for nothing, and manifest nothing. As they say: Be careful what you wish for.

    Many religions speak about a spiritual realm. The Bible covers at least one hundred scriptures about spiritual warfare, thus supporting this dimension outside of our known reality. I do not hear many preachers dive into too much detail, as I assume it's difficult for today's culture to accept it, as the church has a hard enough time getting the basics accepted. But I know these topics are very much on people's minds, which is why I'm trying to cover them in a way that at least opens the door. Until you've had a life experience beyond anything you've ever seen or felt, it's hard to accept this truth, but deep inside, you can feel its presence. We are often afraid to share these weird stories because of fear or doubt or how it might make us look. Knowledge of this spiritual realm doesn't hurt you one bit, but know that, like other things you can't see or comprehend, it doesn't diminish the fact that this realm is real and ever-present.

"Put on the whole armor of God, that you may be able to stand against the schemes of the devil. For we do not wrestle against flesh and blood, but against the rulers, against the authorities, against the cosmic powers over this present darkness, against the spiritual forces of evil in the heavenly places." Ephesians 6:11-12

    Remember that the Bible was written thousands of years ago, and because of changed vocabulary, sometimes we have to decode the message. *Light* could mean positive energy, good, or angel. When you understand this, it opens up insight or clarity for things that are hard to verbalize, as some feelings and experiences have no words to explain.

    I'd have to say that my relationship and faith in my creator is something that I can't fully put into words; it's a collection of words that don't give it justice. It's like a first-time experience, very close to making love for the very first time. All the reading you do, stories you hear, or videos you watch can never substitute the actual feeling. It's the same as giving birth or being present the first time a human enters this world. The feeling inside you is of a glorious energy, something supernatural—the purest forms of life experiences that blow us away. These things happen daily, over and over, forever. People can see you glowing when you're in this state of mind, body, and spirit.

When you align yourself and then align with your creator, your connection becomes very deep and strong. When driven by the Holy Spirit, your presence and aura create a different environment in which others feel and feed off of. This is part of the law of attraction you hear about. Grace, class, swagger, and confidence are appealing. Others want you in their space. They'll say things like, "I don't know, but there's just something about them." It's because there is.

This spiritual realm is a special place with good and bad spirits or energy. When it feels bad, like heat from a fire, move away. I believe we can't see this realm because we wouldn't be able to handle seeing what takes place there.

As we navigate our physical selves through life here on Earth, our spirit in the spiritual realm also navigates a course. When both are in alignment, we find peace with our soul and lives. We find trouble when they get too far off course.

THE LOST ART OF FAITH

When scripture tells us to fear God, it really means, Why do you fear anything else when I am all and can do all for you, to you, and through you? We believe in such petty things in life, but why not in our creator? Why do we doubt Him? We fear or reject something until we learn to respect it or come to understand it. These things are no different than a good parent to a child. We correct our children so worse things don't happen to them. God is no different. We should see God in ourselves; we are created in His image.

Seeing how these truths and principles are interconnected on both a complex and simple scale, it'll open your eyes in a way you may have never experienced before. Once we have the ability to change our perception at will, we can change how the world appears to us. As they say, perception is reality. What you're able to see and accept will be your new reality.

In the movie *The Matrix*, the young boy says to Neo, "It is not the spoon that bends; it is only yourself." The world does not change; it is us that has to do the changing to see the world in a different way.

Chapter 15

My Inspiration

My inspiration comes from a bunch of sources: mother, grandmothers, aunts, ex-wife, friends, bosses, coworkers, Robin Williams, Morgan Freeman, and many movies that speak to me about hope and overcoming major life challenges. When I look at what people have had to go through to get from point A to B, I become inspired to do more myself. At this point, I see the inspiration of God at work through almost everything. I actually hope that when I die, Morgan Freeman is God, because he'd be the coolest dude to hang with and ask all the awesome questions.

During the 1994–1995 Houston Rockets first championship season, Coach Rudy Tomjanovich said, "I have one thing to say to those nonbelievers. Don't ever underestimate the heart of a champion."

THE LOST ART OF FAITH

One of the greatest and saddest movies was *What Dreams May Come* with actor Robin Williams. I feel like after losing my wife, family, and home, that I've lived part of that movie myself. When my girls ask about Heaven, I tell them it's the best of best dreams that you get to live out forever. I know that it will be even better than anything we can comprehend. Maybe it's the sum of joy that's ever been in this universe inside your heart forever.

On the flip side, if you don't believe because you see no benefit, then maybe you'll get nothing but empty space. I don't want to take that gamble because, quite frankly, being a good person of peace, love, and joy based on some faith ain't never gonna hurt no one, ever! That's just simple common sense, which ain't so common these days. My inspiration comes from an internal hope that I also share on Earth as part of who I am, as me. My gift to this planet is hope, inspiration, and motivation to shed some light on something good, and we can all use something good. I know I've survived things on Earth, and I probably shouldn't be here right now, but my work here hasn't been fulfilled. This book, my message, is an inspiration given to me by God.

My grandmother, Geneva Demarest, is my greatest living inspiration. She is currently eighty-six years old, loves me, and believes in me like no one on this planet. Her words have moved me in life, and I now know that's how God speaks to me: through people who have walked this path before me. The advice and encouragement she's given me has shaped some of the greatest moments and achievements of my life. As she fades in life, her spirit grows inside of me so that I may carry the torch in her absence, helping to ground and guide my family when she is no longer here to do that.

She's been through more hell than anyone I know, yet her loving kindness and tender heart penetrate deep inside all that she loves, and her words are powerful like God's because she is the definition of a worthy woman. She's fire and ice, but just and right in all her ways. She has the right balance of hard truth in discipline and putting people in their place, yet she will make sure you know she loves you without condition. She's been my guardian angel here on Earth since I was born, and she always will be.

My personal lord and savior is Jesus Christ. He gave himself so I can have the hope of salvation and grace to someday make it to the kingdom of Heaven—my final destination and true home.

Chapter 16

The Pyramid of Life Concept

When I look at the great pyramids of Egypt, I see some of the world's most amazing superstructures on planet Earth. Since I have an architectural and engineering background, it's even more mind-blowing because I know what we are capable of with today's modern technology. At this point, yes, I'm going off into left field fast, and I'm sure you're thinking, "What in the hell does this have to do with life and success?" Give me a minute, and I shall explain. Life as we know it requires four elements:

- Ourselves (mind, body, spirit)
- Others (relationship, an account, validation)
- Time (a period of time)
- Place (location)

ERIC DUPRE'

The Great Pyramid of Giza has four corners of perfect distance, and from the base to the top, it grows higher, yet gets smaller. Inside are the things of the Pharaoh Khufu's life. The structure, without a doubt, was to be built to last damn near forever. It was not built in vain; it's a message to the future. Just as we make daily choices in life, the stones were placed individually. When one amasses all these choices, we are building an ascending pyramid of life. His life is *inside*, but the *exterior* is the work of this life until the top is reached—the pinnacle or apex of life, ascending as close to Heaven as possible. If a man carefully builds his life based on this model, it would last so others could follow the blueprint he left behind.

In addition to that making logical sense, I feel, without a doubt, that the necessary manpower and resources at that time required something supernatural, or an alien intervention was connected to this ancient superstructure. Either way, the apparent message left behind is a massive symbol with an un-coded meaning.

I share this pyramid story because when I look at God, faith is always interlinked as the creator of all things. The cornerstone of knowledge and wisdom all start when a child seeks these things and the brain is mature enough to begin questioning life with the most powerful three letter word on Earth: Why?

I'm a dyslexic, so I often see things from right to left, just like ancient languages were written. Aramaic and Hebrew ancient biblical text are written from right to left, as were most Egyptian hieroglyphs. If you take "Why?" and read it right to left, you get YHW. YHW is the name of God on ancient Egyptian tombs from 1500–1300 BC and is claimed to be the same as Hebrew Yahweh. YHW God is also found among ancient Sumerians. What does all this mean to the world? Hell, I don't know, but it tells me that the thought and the idea of "Why?" is closely related to our biggest driving desires to know, as it relates to God, our creator.

Chapter 17

Mental Preparedness for Life

At thirty-three years old, most people have gone through enough of life's experiences to fully grasp loss and pain. Reading something versus experiencing it first-hand does not compare. In my opinion, only through experiences can we truly start to understand real-life dynamics of how good and bad moments mold and shape you, though we tend to struggle with the bad times.

If you do not convert your bad experiences into lessons, those experiences will haunt you like a ghost you can't shake. You will not be the first human to experience pain and suffering, and you will not be the last. These events are designed. How prepared you are for them is true power. Take control without fear—only action.

Throughout thousands of basketball practices, Michael Jordan prepared for all kinds of scenarios he'd face at game time, so he was more prepared when others wouldn't have known how to react. He practiced for possibilities. You should conduct the same mental practice, preparing yourself and trying to see the unexpected.

The moment we think something is not possible is the moment we get a Mike Tyson punch to the face and drop to the floor, never knowing what hit us. This doesn't mean you should become a fortune teller; just don't let your guard down to possibilities, and don't allow those thoughts to become worries—just considerations. Allowing your thoughts to run wild could give you great anxiety, which is not what I'm talking about.

The more you acquire from a successful life, the more consideration is needed. It's a numbers game or law of averages. The more kids, responsibilities, and things you have, the more you have to consider. As you get older, things will start to disappear, and this is by design because your focus narrows on the big picture.

When this life ends, a new one that requires only your soul is all you'll take with you. There's a saying: "You never see a U-Haul behind the hearse." This means you can't take anything with you. But I do think you take the collective memories with you, so make them good by living out the best version of you that you can control. Life is designed to condition us for death and the afterlife. We lose animals, grandparents, family, and relationships. What's hard is the lost physical connection and physical sense of love. The love connection doesn't actually go away; it plays on that damn old-emotion button of happiness and sadness. If you truly believe in this amazing afterlife in Heaven, you'll understand *that* is your home, and the absolute best feeling in the world is coming home. Like Dorothy said, "There's no place like home." And she's absolutely right.

When someone dies, understand that they are returning home to be in total peace with absolute love, zero pain, and no fear . . . forever. When you can see such a place for them, you'll understand why it's so important for you to keep your soul intact. This starts with the renewing of the heart and mind toward a righteous, wholesome way of living, with dual positive benefits in two different realms. When your soul is in alignment with your soul in the afterlife, which does not operate in time and place, you'll feel this alignment, because life becomes an easier, peaceful place. Even with all the same old crap that happens, as you align, your ability to stay upright and strong becomes very powerful.

Ecclesiastes 4:9–12 New International Version (NIV)

*⁹Two are better than one,
because they have a good return for their labor:
¹⁰If either of them falls down,
one can help the other up.
But pity anyone who falls
and has no one to help them up.
¹¹Also, if two lie down together, they will keep warm.
But how can one keep warm alone?
¹²Though one may be overpowered,
two can defend themselves.
A cord of three strands is not quickly broken.*

    The beauty of scripture is awesome because it can have multiple hidden meanings until you open your mind to interpretation. The scripture above could be talking about two physical people, or go a little deeper, and you can see that it could very well be talking about a human and God as two. Physically, two can warm each other, but who can warm your heart and soul? When in a relationship with God, He can. Again, the good book states it was written by men, with the inspiration of God.

    I had no clue when I was younger that I'd ever write a book, but once I went through my own spiritual awakening, I felt inspired. I care not how it's interpreted, rather that it helps someone, at any level. As you age and have more experiences, you see different meanings in the same scripture because you have different perspectives. This is spiritual maturity and progress, just like starting as a beginner and becoming a master.

It's also my belief that you will reach a state of maturity that comes full circle, which allows you to enter a purer state of innocence at heart, with knowledge through experience, to obtain a high level of self-control. You're no longer naïve, yet you have compassion for those who lack understanding. You don't judge, instead, showing them an example of how your faith in action has power to resolve or dissolve a negative situation, versus making it worse or leaving it unresolved. These become realized opportunities to use your faith to practice, and to get better.

"Whoever can be trusted with very little can also be trusted with much, and whoever is dishonest with very little will also be dishonest with much." Luke 16:10 (NIV)

This verse is great because it wakes you up to the smaller tests in life. If you can't handle the small tests, what do you think will happen with a bigger test? This is the key to any level of success, from spiritual to business. If you can't do well with $20,000, why in the world would anyone entrust you with more? Logic meets scripture very well in this simple verse.

Hopefully by now you're seeing the pattern I'm using with breaking down the logical lessons of the scripture so you can understand how to better utilize its meanings and lessons. As you remember various scriptures, when a situation arises, this is where some of the magic happens because you'll automatically snap to your current situation and marry it with scripture to counter it through actions and words.

It's hard to attack any righteous man in public if the other person has impure intentions. This is being meek, which again is when you use power, under control, for righteousness. I've seen a small man speak truth to an enraged person, and with strong eye contact and an unthreatening body language and tone of voice, defuse the bomb, so to speak. When another man has the courage and wisdom to do that among other men, it commands high regard and is a true leadership quality. And men with good leadership qualities tend to be more successful.

Chapter 18

Patterns

What's in your heart? Good? Bad? Evil? A combo? The more good you have, the more positive you'll be, because what's in your heart, the mind is surely to follow.

"Guard your heart above all else, for it determines the course of your life." Proverbs 4:23

The mother of all equations for a successful life through your faith is Faith=Success. Here's the process and breakdown:

Heart (Passion and desires): The driving force of all of your intentions—good, bad, or evil.
Thought: What you're thinking about doing. All of your choices in life pass through this door before any action can ever take place. Conscious and subconscious doesn't matter.

Your choices come from your mind. Once you're an adult, you are the programmer of your mind, and at this point, you can't turn back, as you are now responsible for all of your thoughts and actions. Free will and choice start here. If you want to be truly free, you must free your mind.

Emotions and Feelings: These coincide with your thoughts, and you are also in full control. If you're not, someone else sure as hell will be. I can do things to provoke you or influence you, but at the end of the day, *you* will always be in charge of your emotions and feelings. Keep calm. Mind over matter and mind over emotions take practice.

Why do you think soldiers are yelled at in their face? It's to break them of reacting out of emotion. Words are just words. You can tune them out or choose to keep them inside, but it's a choice in which you have full control over. To fully master emotional reactions, you must overcome dealing with your deepest fears in all situations. The devil uses fear to control you like a puppet.

"What doesn't kill you will make you stronger." Unfortunately, this statement is true and means going through painful experiences to show you what you're made of. Fear is the worst of all the emotions and feelings, and is the one we should work on the most to gain control over our fears. Later,

I'll cover addressing fear, as it extremely important to this process and this book's solution to the reader.

Action: What comes out of your mouth, the expressions on your face, the control of your arms and legs . . . this is all you. Actions and reactions are domino effects.

Sometimes, doing nothing is best. You yield zero energy, and you force the other person to make a bad choice that they will have to live with. Self-control and knowing thyself is the key here. You know what triggers your emotional reactions, and once you know the triggers, you can start taking back control of you. Once an action is in motion, there is no undoing or redoing it. This is the final and last level in which you and your life will be defined by the total sum of your life's actions and reactions. If you repeat bad habits through your actions, what do you think your life will look like? If you repeat good or better habits, what do you think your life will look? Bingo! It's about making better choices over bad ones. No one's perfect and never will be. Perfection never teaches you like failure does, but at some point, we must get out of the revolving door of failure by once again making a single choice.

Reaction/Chain Reaction: Your actions become chain reactions. When you pump out good things into the universe, they return to the source. When you pump out bad, they also return to the source. This is karma. Your negative energy and bad habits can drain the hell out of other people. So stop that!

Negative/Positive Aftermath Results of Actions/Reactions: After a while, your negative energy can drain people so much, they won't want anything to do with you. Their body's subconscious will perceive you as a threat and start to reject you. So even if someone loves you deeply but you can't change a draining bad habit, that person's inner spirit forces them to get away from the threat. This is very much like when a pregnant woman is dying. The body will try to force her into labor so the baby has a chance to live. The human body's brain, or computer, has tons of programs prewired in to keep it safe or to sustain life. I don't mean in the physical sense. If your spirit and heart are dead from zero motivation because something or someone causes unhappiness, your spirit will also go into fight-or-flight mode. The closer you run to the person you hurt, the more the spirit wants to safeguard itself. You can keep your body alive, but if your spirit is dead, you're truly not living a happy life.

If there is a fire for something deep in your heart, it will bleed out of you like an unstoppable madman. You will eat, live, and breathe it. It will manifest from a dream to your reality. As long as you have the best intensions inside your heart and you convert your mind and align it with your creator's greater purpose for you, my friend, you will live a successful life by way of your newfound faith.

It's taken me thirty-nine years of questioning and living through this process to formulate this conclusion. I never once said it will be easy or that speedbumps or detours will not happen; they will. Bad crap happens to good people every day, but that doesn't give you the right to toss that junk onto other people. You may have an illness that makes controlling your emotions and actions hard, but you can always control your character. How you treat others in this world is how they will treat and judge you.

If you handle your character with class and not spread your hate, pain, or anger, you, my friend, are honorable. You are worthy of the highest praise, and if you don't get everything you ever wanted here on Earth, I assure you that making these changes in your heart and lifestyle will give you everything in another life.

If you choose to stay on your current path, just ask yourself how far it's gotten you and if you have real peace, love, and joy in your cold dead heart from not loving others—even when it's hard. You want someone to love you even when you don't deserve it, right? If we don't act more like the Son of God, and instead of the son of man, we will be denied at the gates because our hearts and souls are directed toward yourself and worldly things first. If we treat God's children like crap and don't give forgiveness to those who don't deserve grace, then why in the hell would our father do the same for us when we are in need of it and equally don't deserve it?

I found out a long time ago about the word *deserve*. It's a stupid word when used in the singular sense. It has nothing to do with changing your character for the better and making the most of what you have. That's life. We don't get to choose where, how, when, to whom, or to what circumstances we come into in this tough world. When that reality sets in, you just have to dig in and start making some positive changes for a righteous and better way of living for yourself and all the people you encounter.

> *"Ask, and it shall be given to you; seek, and ye shall find; knock, and it shall be opened unto you: For everyone that asketh receiveth; and he that seeketh findeth; and to him that knocketh, it shall be opened." Mathew 7:7-8*

Just imagine choosing a better life and seeing it come to fruition. Now imagine that you lead your younger self by example—they are someone you can now pass this wisdom onto.

What you leave behind is important because when you die and go to Heaven, time has no limits. All your tiny ripples in the pond shape the future of this world—directly and indirectly. Can you imagine being around to see such a thing? Limitless dreams of the greatest things and lives you can image being a part of? I know we can manifest things here on

Earth, and surely even more in another place, but if you don't have faith or beliefs here, how can you manifest more in a place you don't believe in?

What does it cost to believe in all this? Absolutely nothing. This is one of the greatest gifts our creator could give us: eternal peace, love, and joy that have no boundaries and are only limited by what you can believe.

I believe the entire universe was created by something powerful, so what prevents His powers from creating my Heaven? Absolutely nothing. In the end, if we live a successful, righteous, and good life here on Earth, using a sound doctrine of living, what do we have to lose?

Chapter 19

Bad Programming Equals Bad Output, Every Time

Humans are like machines controlled by a CPU. If we reverse engineer this concept, you'll see exactly what I'm talking about.

Everything you do is always a thought first. It may happen so quickly, or you think it's without thinking, but it's not. You are pre-programmed to react based on programs hardwired in your conscious and subconscious. They pass through your brain before the physical body is told what to do. This is a fact. Bad programs are just bad habits, or apps, running in the background. The bad programs consume memory and energy, and they drain you.

ERIC DUPRE'

I like to use the computer terms (*hard drive, OS, RAM, power source, programs, background programs*) because that seems to be a great visual for people. The computer is patterned off the human's brain, so we are like computers in many ways. That's why you hear terms like *mind hacking*. If you have bipolarism, depression, or PTSD, you have viruses, or bad programs. Mind over matter is beautiful because your brain, unlike a computer, is organic matter that can actually change if you can figure out how to hack into yourself.

People say, "Well, I am who I am, and that's it." Since that's what they believe, why would they change? You are who you *think* you are or what you *think* you can be, and you and only you have control over that. There are limits for some, but when I talk about the masses, you control you. What you say or don't say, when you say it, and how you say it can make the difference of being an average Joe versus a millionaire. I feel that those who can grasp and are open to this concept have no limits to what they can achieve. Intelligence and wisdom are attributed to those who can harness knowledge and experience for self-advancement.

"Do not conform to the pattern of this world but be transformed by the renewing of your mind. Then you will be able to test and approve what God's will is—his good, pleasing and perfect will."
Romans 12:2

THE LOST ART OF FAITH

I could use this scripture over and over throughout this book because it's a major component, written right here in plain ol' scripture. You think it's a coincidence that biblical text is called *scripture* and computer coding is call *script*? I don't. *Script* and *scripture* are just different forms of coding something. Once you learn how to code or decode, you're off to the races. Be transformed by the renewing of your mind.

The good book was written over two thousand years ago. I personally find parts of the Bible to be boring, but I'm breaking out sections to give you the Cliff Notes version. This should really shift your openness to what the Bible is here for. It being so old and applying to humans in 2019 blows my mind. This ain't no joke of a book. I personally wasn't there, nor was anyone else alive today, so I never argue the historical facts. I only argue facts that are toward real application of producing a good human on this planet. The closer you are in alignment with its lessons, the better off you'll be, even if that's just a state of mind since your perception is your true reality.

So, if you could hack your brain and make yourself believe every day was the best day of your life, would you do it? Duh, we all would. And that's part of the Bible's power. It's part of the blueprints left for us. It gives us historical events of what typically happens when folks get out of alignment. Bad stuff happens, so you can argue and fight about it or take some effort and try it like I did.

Yeah, I had my deep reservations about all this, as well. I'm a mega-driven, analytical, quantitative, logical person by nature, which is why I'm taking the time to write this book as a connect-the-dots breakdown for you, even though I can't make you understand and feel the same way I do. The transformation is an experience *you* need to feel. Once you experience it, only then will you truly understand what your faith means for you. I've never felt another power like the Holy Spirit. It's an energy source of all things you can't explain but just feel inside you. This is called "The God Code." Science shows these nano-patterns in all matter and all things.

What I've come to learn is that God does not play by our rules, thus time does not exist to him. We can be one millisecond from discovering or destroying everything, and he can push it one thousand years further out or reset it to 1999, and we'd never know. This is the carrot-and-horse trick, and God has been playing that game since the first "Why?" came out of man's mouth. Universal truths and patterns all tie in together.

The science, math, logic, and the spiritual are unseen but interlinked, just like you and I are linked through our parents. We can go backwards from that point to the time of creation. What's amazing is science is now proving that black space, once considered nothing, is something. The fact that we even give *nothing* a name means it's something because we've identified its existence. This is no different than your own acknowledgment of faith and of yourself.

    I hope you enjoyed reading this book and that, to some degree, it helps you solve internal struggles so you may live a happier, better life. I wrote this to help lost, broken, struggling people—like myself—find hope and inspiration to heal and restore hope back into their lives. I hope to help you solve or resolve the loss of love for life or the loss of loved ones, mental health, PTSD, depression. I hope to help you find faith, find your way back from being lost, find real answers and solutions to deep questions, and find purpose and meaning. We don't get to choose our birth or our death; we just get to choose what that dash in between represents during our time on this planet.

    I hope I choose more good than bad and bring more good than bad into this world. I guess we'll all just have to wait to find out.

Chapter 20

Selling Your Soul

For the first time in my life, I'm actually gonna say that selling out is a good thing—but not in the way you might think. If you're going to sell your soul, make sure you sell out to the right buyer. To allow God's power to change your life, you have to completely sell out to him and trust that he knows best. Surely, the creator of the universe knows best, as he knows all.

A friend once said this: "To be made new, we have to be destroyed." He was correct, but you have to understand there may be a trade-off or cost you must pay. I believe you must be willing to lose everything to gain it all back as promised. The promise doesn't say when. Let me say that again: the promise doesn't say when. If you're willing to let go of this entire world for me, I will keep my promise. So just let go, or at some point, it will be ripped away from you.

The money says it all: "In God We Trust." The fear of letting go is so hard for man, but for those who can, they will be rewarded beyond what they can dream. The cost is always high for things of great value. What are you willing to give up?

THE LOST ART OF FAITH

Your life is already His, so that's not the bargaining chip. It must be a sacrifice of something you love more than yourself. But know that in doing this, at some point, it will all be returned to you, tenfold. Maybe here on Earth. May in the afterlife. Who knows? No one truly knows. That's why it's called *faith*.

If you amassed everything on Earth but would die in eighty to one hundred years, what would you have truly amassed? Nothing. You're dead, and you believed in only yourself, thus you'll die alone by yourself—if that's what you want and want to believe in. I didn't create myself or this universe, and I owe my life to God. He just wants me to acknowledge and respect him as if he were just a man, which is how we should treat every man. We show Him our love and respect by treating others as if they were God himself. After reading this, you may look at people differently, as they are all His creation, which means they are all His children. When you mess with a father or mothers' child, be prepared to pay the price.

These same principles apply to God's children. The golden rule is treating others as you wish to be treated, but the problem is some people treat themselves like crap, so they follow this rule as a lower standard, as one might have a higher standard of expectation. You'll never control that person, but you will control you for the sake of pleasing God.

ERIC DUPRE'

When we try to control God's natural order by worldly methods, we cause Him to offset this at a more rapid pace, which is why the world seems to have sped up and is moving faster. Our intelligence thinks we can outthink natural order and process, and when we lose respect for this order, He normally allows us to drop the hammer on ourselves. Sometimes we must be decent and sacrifice pride for order.

To keep a good relationship, it's often better to keep an ally than to prove your strength or your point. When our ego and pride—out of the glory of our own might—overshadow our grace and compassion, it reveals our true character. To humble yourself before someone or something more powerful than you is a sign of great meekness. Meekness is power under control. When you know you're more powerful than someone else, you don't have to prove it to anyone unless you fear them.

Submitting to God is an honor, as your submitting to the attorney of the most powerful being in the known universe. Just ask yourself if you can create an entire universe. If the answer is no, then who would ever fault you for that? No one. So never worry about what mortals think when you praise a true God.

There's nothing embarrassing about paying respect to a higher authority, just like there's nothing wrong with respecting a manager, CEO, boss, general, president, mother, father, or teacher. If you can respect these people in public, surely you can respect God.

⁵ "When Jesus had entered Capernaum, a centurion came to him, asking for help. ⁶ "Lord," he said, "my servant lies at home paralyzed, suffering terribly."

⁷ Jesus said to him, "Shall I come and heal him?"

⁸ The centurion replied, "Lord, I do not deserve to have you come under my roof. But just say the word, and my servant will be healed. ⁹ For I myself am a man under authority, with soldiers under me. I tell this one, 'Go,' and he goes; and that one, 'Come,' and he comes. I say to my servant, 'Do this,' and he does it."

¹⁰ When Jesus heard this, he was amazed and said to those following him, "Truly I tell you, I have not found anyone in Israel with such great faith. ¹¹ I say to you that many will come from the east and the west and will take their places at the feast with Abraham, Isaac and Jacob in the kingdom of Heaven. ¹² But the subjects of the kingdom will be thrown outside, into the darkness, where there will be weeping and gnashing of teeth."

¹³ Then Jesus said to the centurion, "Go! Let it be done just as you believed it would." And his servant was healed at that moment."
Matthew 8:5–13

When you have real faith and believe in it, God's authority works. When you only believe when you want something to serve yourself, it just doesn't work. You can keep trying your own way and see how far this gets you in life, but again, if you're only living for this life, you might want to think about what forever would feel and look like. Seriously, really think and contemplate that reality and ask yourself: Can I serve the kingdom of God and get a good life here on Earth? The answer is yes, and this understanding allows you to open the door to the real power of faith.

Chapter 21

Final Thoughts and Conclusion

Without a doubt, the message is about man's search for an absolute truth and answer to enlightenment. Once found, man no longer needs to validate himself, his being, or his actions in comparison to others. You add things you love to your life by choice, not out of void or a need to complete you, but to enhance you. If something doesn't enhance your life, it needs to go.

     Faith is an unshakeable trust and confidence in someone or something. Throughout this book, I've used the term *your faith*. It's not my faith, not your spouse's, not your mama's, not your spiritual leader's, but your own personal faith you have developed. I've laid out tons of crap that will distract you in life and how to possibly counter or avoid these distractions, and how you can obtain and draw closer to your faith and beliefs in life. This will help you nail that down and live more freely and unrestricted, with confidence, and without excuses or doubt.

You will be the one who still walks the walk, but it's my that hope I've shed some light from where you are now, back to the road. From there, she's all yours. Knowing you're on the right path gives you peace and lets you finally breathe again. When you can stop asking why, why, and why and just live, live, live, your day will be filled. You will soak in life versus going nowhere and battling a mental labyrinth of confusion.

If I've done my job, the book doesn't end here, as we are links in an invisible chain in which we can collectively share more insight. I and others want to hear your story and thoughts about this message. Hope is what we need to leave accessible as our greatest gift to the next generation. Losing hope in my faith is just not possible. Life has tried to take that from me at all costs, and it couldn't.

I don't know if that's a gift or a curse, but something in this world wanted to take my hope and faith away from me, as if it was in danger of me spreading hope. In my heart, I have unconditional love for mankind. Anything bad is out of frustration, caused by inner pain and demons. I have accepted my cross as a sinner, hypocrite, and a failed man, but our creator is a father, just like me, and I love my kids. No matter how bad they screw up, they can always come home to me, as I will never give up on them, even when they give up on themselves.

Most of us don't understand the power we have inside ourselves, but when another knows this power, it's possible to light that flame. This is why they say patience is a virtue. Good things come to those who wait; not those who give up because it's hard and takes time.

I shall fear no man but God, and though I walk in the valley and shadow of darkness, I will fear no evil. Simply put, you can give into fear. and you will be controlled by that fear your entire life. You will not live the successful, happy life you deserve until you kill your demons, fears, and obstacles that are in your way. If you can learn to beat your toughest opponent—yourself—and create your own faith, you can then help your loved ones do the same and truly leave something behind for this world.

How will you truly ever know if you're on the right track in life? When you wake up in the morning and have excitement instead of anxiety about your day—even if that excitement is something small. With effort, you can start to change each part of your life until each portion is in place for you to be happy and satisfied. It won't be perfect, and it won't ever be fully complete, but it will be good.

If you can reach this stage of your life and sustain it, knowing you'll beat struggles like you have up to this point, you're good. You're now walking and living in your faith. The automatic habits start to produce great fruits of this labored task we call life. Be well, live well, and this gift and knowledge shall flow through you in this world. In the end, we have free will in our beliefs and choices. Choices often require hardship, because doing right isn't about taking the easy way. Staying the course, even when all hope seems lost, is a true testament of a man's faith. The scripture below says it best.

"For the gate is narrow and the way is hard that leads to life, and those who find it are few." Mathew 7:14

As I finish with the closing words of this book, I am completely exhausted with life at this point. But this is when you know you've left everything on the field of battle and did the best you knew how at that time. When your father has seen you give your all and fight like hell, the door will open. I see God's hand at work, and inspiration is in all things, good and bad. I never thought I'd get past ten pages, but the Holy Spirit carried me through most of this, by my own willpower. Without faith, I would have quit and given up a long time ago.

If I can say "I love you" as a broken man, then surely your creator and your true father loves you just like a mother who has given birth and is holding her child in her arms for the very first time. Again, the best words that I can use to describe how much your creator loves you and wants a better life for you is through scriptures left behind for us.

Avery and Riley,

Daddy loves y'all very much, and I want y'all to know I'll never give up, and I'll never stop fighting because I love y'all more than myself or anything in this world.

> *"Anything is possible if a person believes."*
> **Mark 9:23**

Quick References for Quotes & Scripture

Psalm 77

You promised me, Lord, that if I followed you, you would walk with me always. But I have noticed that during the most trying periods of my life there has only been one set of footprints in the sand. Why, when I needed you most, have you not been there for me?"
The Lord replied, "The years when you have seen only one set of footprints, my child, is when I carried you."

Romans 12:2

Do not conform to the pattern of this world but be transformed by the renewing of your mind. Then you will be able to test and approve what God's will is—his good, pleasing and perfect will.

Mathew 16:26

"To gain the world but lose one's soul."

George S. Patton Jr

"If everyone is thinking alike, then somebody isn't thinking."

Benjamin Franklin

"If you fail to plan, you are planning to fail."

Eric J. Dupre'

"If it's good, it's a blessing, and if it's bad, it's just a lesson."

Albert Einstein

"It's not that I'm so smart, it's just that I stay with the problems longer."

DMX

"See, to live is to suffer. But to survive... Well, that's to find meaning in the suffering."

Ephesians 2:8

For by grace you have been saved through fate, and that not of yourselves; it is the gift of God, Not of works, lest anyone should boast.

2 Timothy 3:16

"All scripture is given by inspiration of God, and is profitable for doctrine, for reproof, correction, for instruction in righteousness."

Proverbs 4:23

Guard your heart above all else, for it determines the course of your life.

Ecclesiastes 4:9-12

Two are better than one,

because they have a good return for their labor:

If either of them falls down,

one can help the other up.

But pity anyone who falls

and has no one to help them up.

Also, if two lie down together, they will keep warm.

But how can one keep warm alone?

Though one may be overpowered,

two can defend themselves.

Luke 16:10

"Whoever can be trusted with very little can also be trusted with much, and whoever is dishonest with very little will also be dishonest with much."

Proverbs 12:1

Whoever loves discipline loves knowledge, but whoever hates correction is **stupid**.

Unknown

"Failure isn't fatal and success isn't final but it's the courage to continue that counts."

1 Corinthians 14:20

"Brothers do not be children in your thinking. Be infants in evil, but in your thinking be mature."

Luke 6:31

"Treat others in the same way that you would want them to treat you."

Mathew 7:7-8

Ask, and it shall be given you; seek, and ye
shall find; knock, and it shall be opened unto you:
For everyone that asketh receiveth; and he that seeketh
findeth; and to him that knocketh it shall be opened.

Mathew 7:14

For the gate is narrow and the way is hard that leads to life, and those who find it are few.

www.ingramcontent.com/pod-product-compliance
Lightning Source LLC
Chambersburg PA
CBHW060859170526
45158CB00001B/419